Watercolour
Interiors

Watercolour
Interiors

Projects, Tips and Techniques

General Editor: Richard Taylor

amber
BOOKS

First published in 2006 by
Amber Books Ltd
Bradley's Close
74–77 White Lion Street
London N1 9PF
www.amberbooks.co.uk

ISBN-13: 978-1-904687-70-2
ISBN-10: 1-904687-70-9

Distributed in the UK by
Bookmart Ltd
Blaby Road
Wigston
Leicester LE18 4SE

Contributing Artists:
George Cousins: 52–57; Abi Edgar: 28–33; Sharon Finmark: 17–21, 22–27; George Lidzay: 41–46, 90–96; John Palmer: 65–71; George Raynes: 58–64; Tom Robb: 72–77, 78–83; Ian Sidaway: 6–10, 84–89; Adrian Smith: 34–40; Tig Sutton: 11–16; Albany Wiseman: 47–51

Picture Credits:
DeAgostini/George Taylor

Printed in Singapore

Contents

Underwater swimmer

*Full of life and movement, this unusual picture of a swimmer
gliding through the water is a combination of watercolour and collage.*

S wimming pools are full of colour and pattern. Ripples play across the water and light catches the splashes, producing a sparkling effect. This makes for an interesting painting subject.

This composition focuses on a single swimmer gliding just below the surface of the water. The movement of the water distorts the appearance of the tiled pool floor and the swimmer's body, giving rise

▼ **Paint and torn paper complement each other in this graphic representation of a streamlined figure in the water.**

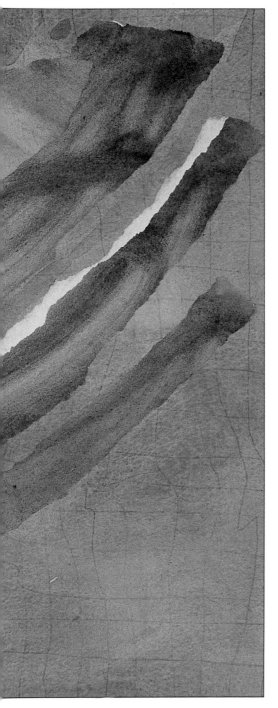

to unexpected, fluid shapes. The light hitting and reflecting off both the water and the figure creates a distinctive patterned effect that lends itself to being reproduced in blocks of colour.

Paint and paper

Watercolour and collage are combined in this step-by-step to create an interesting textured painting. The paint is applied in stages wet-on-dry, each layer building up the strength of colour. Once you've mixed a wash, add a little more of one or other of the colours as you paint to avoid

a uniform look. You could also add a little gum arabic to the mixes to intensify the colour, but this is up to you.

Apply the collage once the painting is complete, using painted watercolour papers. When tearing shapes, try to capture the general movement of the water and the patterns on the swimmer. Due to the weave of the paper, tearing in one direction will produce a white edge, whereas if you tear the other way you'll get a coloured edge. Use this to your advantage by letting the white edges represent ripples catching the light.

FIRST STEPS

1 ▲ **Draw the main elements** Using a 2B pencil, outline the figure of the swimmer and draw the tiles on the base of the swimming pool. Notice how the rippling water distorts the tiles into a pattern of undulating lines.

2 ▲ **Begin painting** Mix cadmium lemon yellow and brown madder watercolour. Using a No. 7 round brush, wash this over the figure. Darken the mix with brown madder and permanent mauve, and paint mid tones on the body, leaving bands of pale tone showing through.

3 ▶ Add dark tones

Add ultramarine to the brown mix to make a purplish-brown for the hair; dilute for the pattern of dark tones on the figure. Extend the fingers to give an impression of movement. Block in the swimsuit with the cadmium lemon; add brown madder for the shadow. Mix Payne's grey and burnt umber to make a dark tone for the hair and the right eye.

4 ▼ Block in the water

Mix Payne's grey and ivory black. Changing to a 6mm (¼in) flat brush, paint stripes on the swimsuit. Make a dilute wash of cobalt turquoise and cerulean blue. Wash over the pool with a No. 12 round.

Express yourself

A change of format

Combining paint with collage is fun, so why not try another composition in the same vein? Here, the swimmer glides down the paper, creating a vertical line that leads to a circle of ripples. Her shadow on the tiles is a distorted version of her body shape and gives depth to the water. Texture is built up with collage shapes, as in the step-by-step, but the watercolour is more subdued.

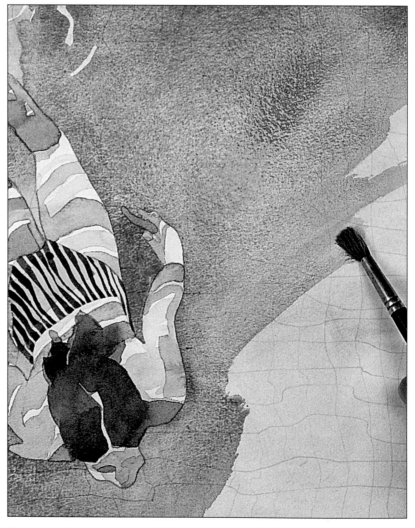

5 ▲ Paint the water pattern

Make a stronger mix of the two blues and paint the pattern made by the moving water on the left, leaving some of the undercolour showing. On the right, completely cover the undercolour.

DEVELOPING THE PICTURE

You have now laid the foundation for the collage. Before you begin, paint papers with colours that correspond to those of the swimmer and water: a dark and a pale blue, a dark and a pale flesh tone, and a dark hair colour.

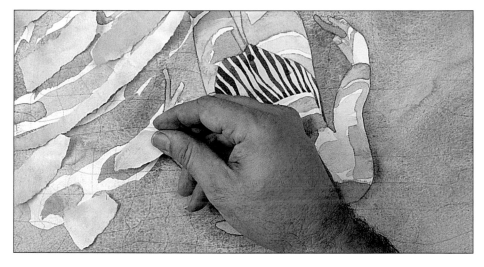

6 ▲ **Arrange pale blue shapes** Tear a piece of pale blue painted paper (see Expert Advice, below) into a variety of strips and patches that correspond with the pattern of light and ripples on the water. Arrange the torn paper shapes on the painting – some pieces can overlap the swimmer's body.

7 ▶ **Glue the ripples** Spray adhesive on to the back of the pale blue shapes and stick them in position. You can butt shapes up to the body by cutting long strips with a scalpel. Either cut them directly on the paper, or if you prefer, mark a line with the pencil, then use the scalpel on a cutting mat.

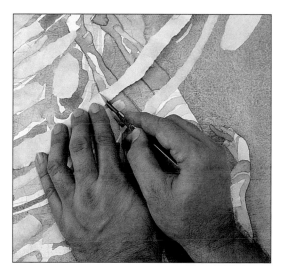

EXPERT ADVICE
Prepare collage papers

Choose a variety of papers for the collage – firm, slightly textured ones are best. Using a No. 12 round brush, paint the papers loosely, working in all directions and allowing the brush marks to show so that you create an interesting surface (as shown right).

8 ▼ **Add to the collage** Tear some dark blue paper into curved bands and glue them on the right. Now tear small patches and strips of paper in dark flesh and hair shades; place them on the legs, shoulders and hair. Make some fit the body contours, but extend others to suggest the distorting effect of the water.

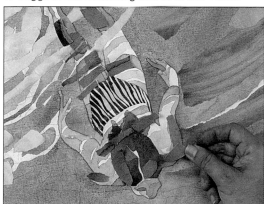

9 ▼ **Stick on pale colours** Stick small strips of pale, flesh-coloured paper on the legs, feet, shoulders and back to add highlights. Finally, glue tiny scraps of white paper in the top left of the picture to represent dappled light.

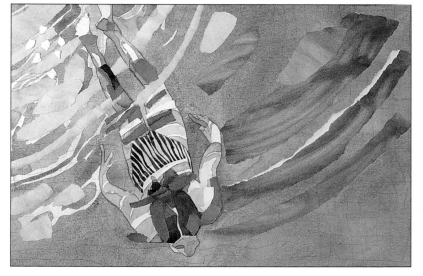

A FEW STEPS FURTHER

The collage is now complete and cleverly plays up the textural and patterned elements in the picture. To blend the collage into the painting a little, add some more touches of watercolour here and there.

10 ▶ **Work on the water** Using the stronger blue wash from step 5, paint some ripples in the water, taking the brush marks right across the arms and legs. Splatter drops of dark blue to the left of the swimmer.

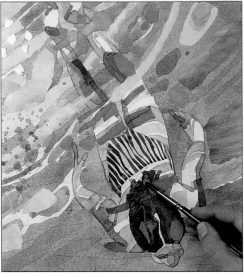

11 ▲ **Add definition** With stronger mixes of the hair and flesh colours from the palette, paint shadows on the hair and limbs. Define the right eye, and the fingers, heels and toes.

THE FINISHED PICTURE

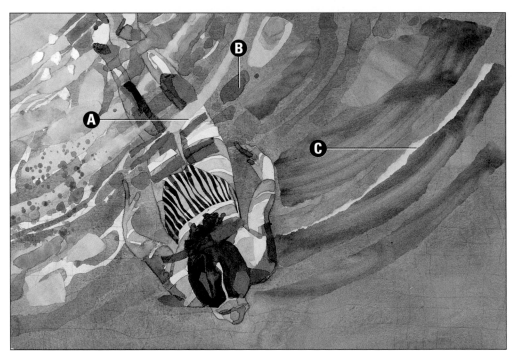

A Raised texture
Torn from a range of medium-weight watercolour papers, the stuck-down shapes add texture to the smooth, flat surface of the underpainting.

B Wet-on-dry
Each layer of paint was left to dry before the next was applied, so the blocks of colours have well-defined edges that complement the patterns made by the collage.

C Torn edge
The uneven white edge of one of the torn pieces of collage paper is left unpainted to suggest a ripple catching the light in the swimming pool.

Inside the study

Watercolour is a flexible medium which can create many different effects. The 'one-stroke' wet-on-dry method gives crisp, clean images.

◀ **The simple geometric shapes of the books and box are brightly lit from one side to give emphatic shadows.**

The true beauty of watercolour painting is seen when it is applied layer upon layer as areas of pure colour. The building up of layers of translucent washes gives the painting a lovely, luminous brilliance.

The key to producing clear, vibrant watercolours is to keep the washes fresh and clean, and to allow each wash to dry thoroughly before you lay the next. This is called the wet-on-dry technique. Working in this way you can build up layers of fresh, jewel-like colour.

Working light to dark

When using pure watercolour, you do not have the option of adding a lighter tone over a dark tone, so the lightest tone available is the white of the paper. Plan the way you will work before you start. Look for the brightest highlights on your objects and make sure you retain these as white paper. You need to work 'light to dark' in the classic watercolour way, laying down the lightest tones of the local colours first, then gradually building up the tones by overlaying successive washes of colour.

Keep your colours fresh

Choose a large palette with many recesses, or use several saucers, so that you can keep each wash separate. Have two jars of water, one for rinsing your brushes and the other for diluting the paint for the wash, and change the water fairly frequently.

FIRST STROKES

1 ▼ **Locate the main elements** Using a 4B pencil, locate the objects on the sheet, starting in the middle and working outwards. Use very light lines to provide a guide for the rest of the drawing. Refine the drawing, checking vertical and horizontal alignments, angles and 'negative shapes'. Include the outlines of the cast shadows.

2 ▶ **Lay the first pale pink washes** Make a pale wash of permanent rose toned down with a touch of Payne's grey. Test the wash on scrap paper and add more water if the colour is too intense. Apply to the top book with a No. 6 brush. Add scarlet to the wash to produce a warmer red for the second book. Leave to dry.

3 ◀ **Establish the box and blue books** Mix a wash of burnt umber with a touch of scarlet and Payne's grey. Using the No. 6 brush, apply the paint to the front and sides of the box. Add a little cobalt blue to create a cooler brown for the top. Make a dilute cobalt blue wash with a touch of Payne's grey to paint the book on the top of the pile. Using the very tip of the brush, take the wash around the golden lettering.

EXPERT ADVICE
Leaving gaps between areas of wash

To keep the image crisp, it is important to prevent colours running into each other. Do this by drying each patch of colour thoroughly before you progress to the adjoining areas. If this is too slow, you can save time by leaving a sliver of paper unpainted between adjacent areas of colour – the wash will not bleed across the dry paper.

▶ **A cool red (permanent rose) and a warm red (scarlet) will give you just the right colour for the reddest books.**

4 ▲ **Begin to paint the surface** Continue blocking in the blue books with a slightly more intense version of the colour. Leave the painting to dry. Mix a wash of raw sienna with a touch of cadmium yellow and light red. Block in the golden colour of the supporting surface, then leave it to dry.

5 ▲ **Paint the background** Mix a very pale greenish-yellow for the background. Use lemon yellow with a little cobalt blue and raw sienna. Lay this on as a single flat wash. Leave to dry.

DEVELOPING THE PICTURE

At this point all the elements of the picture have been established. Now you need to build up the darker tones with more intense versions of the initial washes. This will give the image a three-dimensional quality.

6 ▼ **Add dark tones** Mix a wash of permanent rose with a touch of burnt umber for the shaded spine of the top red book. Use the tip of the brush to lay a thin line of colour along the top edge of the cover. Add a touch of burnt umber to a wash of scarlet for the shaded parts of the second book. Notice the soft edge where the shaded area meets the light area – dip your brush in water and run it along the edge of the wash. For the shaded side of the box, use burnt sienna darkened with Payne's grey.

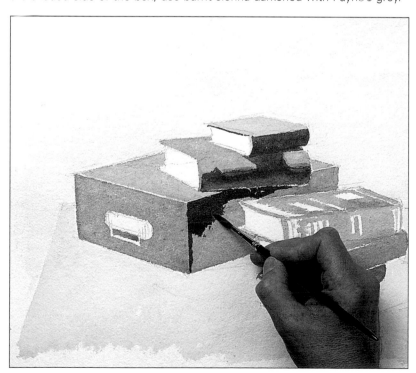

USE A HAIR-DRYER TO SPEED UP DRYING

TROUBLESHOOTER

To retain the integrity of each layer of wash, it is important that the painting is thoroughly dry before you apply successive washes. This can take time. A hair-dryer will speed things up. Don't use a dryer if there are puddles of wash, and choose a low setting – this avoids runnels of paint being blown across the support.

7 ▲ **Add more dark tones to the spines** Darken cobalt blue with Payne's grey. Using this wash, apply colour to the spine of the blue books, working carefully around the golden lettering on the spine.

◄ **Use permanent rose with a touch of Payne's grey for the cooler of the red books.**

► **Mix Payne's grey, burnt umber and raw sienna to create a dark but warm tone for the cast shadows.**

8 ▼ **Add the cast shadows** The shadows that fall on the supporting surface are important to establish the horizontal plane on which the objects are resting. Paint them with a wash of Payne's grey with burnt umber and raw sienna, using the No. 6 brush. Work carefully to create crisp edges. Leave to dry.

9 ▼ **Erase pencil lines** Using the previous wash, lay bands of shadow along the edge of the book covers. Leave to dry. Erase any distracting pencil lines with a kneadable rubber.

Express yourself
Editing and simplifying

The colours, shapes and textures in a subject are merely a jumping-off point for the artist. The 'picture-making' process involves manipulating, editing and emphasizing to create an image that is effective and unique. Here the subject has been simplified, which emphasizes the shapes of the objects, the pattern made by the light tone on the ends of the books, and the way this is echoed by the areas of shade and shadow. Try stripping your still-life subject down to its bare essentials and see what emerges.

10 ▲ **Add details to the box handle** Use a Payne's grey/burnt umber mix to paint the brass handle, leaving the white of the paper for the highlights. Use the tip of the brush and don't worry about precise details – a simplified version will be very convincing.

11 ▶ **Start to add the darker tones to the books** Apply a mix of permanent rose with Payne's grey to the cover of the top book, leaving a sliver of underlying colour along the edge, where light catches it. For the second book cover, apply permanent rose with scarlet.

12 ▲ **Work up details** At this point, decide which areas need to be emphasized. Warm up the side of the box that is turned to the light with a wash of burnt sienna and use the tip of the brush to add a few details to the handle. Mix cobalt blue and Payne's grey and add dark tones to the tops of the blue books, using the tip of the brush to work around the lettering.

A FEW STEPS FURTHER

The two most difficult stages in creating a picture are getting started and deciding when it is finished. The painting is complete and entirely convincing, but you might want to take it further, adding emphasis and detail.

13 ▲ **Developing the surface** The contrast between the objects and the supporting surface is a little stark. Rectify this with a flat wash of raw sienna and burnt sienna. Leave to dry. Intensifying this area pulls the entire image together. Add a wash of raw sienna with Payne's grey to the end of the bottom blue book.

14 ▲ **Adding gold lettering** The covers of the books are blocked with gold lettering. You can suggest this simply by going over the white lettered areas with raw sienna toned down with a tiny touch of Payne's grey.

15 ▲ **Warm the top of the box** Add warmth to the top of the wooden box by adding a final wash of burnt umber and burnt sienna. This final layer of colour will add both depth and warmth.

16 ▲ **Enrich the handle** Develop the brass handle further by working into it with Payne's grey warmed with burnt umber. A few touches will be surprisingly effective. Use this mix to add details and lettering on the covers of the red books.

THE FINISHED PICTURE

A Layers of crisp colour
Dry each application of watercolour before you apply the next – watercolour applied wet on dry is much easier to control.

B Small details are important
Small, generalized details, such as the scrollwork on the handle of the box, can add character and richness to a painting.

C Working light to dark
With pure watercolour you do not have a white to create light tones. The white of the paper is the lightest local colour – here, the pages of the book.

Relaxing inside the house

Cool blues, mauves, pinks and greys, enlivened with touches of brighter colour, create the right mood for this tranquil study.

This relaxed study shows off the versatility of the watercolour medium. Working with wet-in-wet washes, colours have drifted into each other to suggest the luxurious texture and the fall of the velvet throws on the sofa.

And these large expanses of colour contrast effectively with the more detailed study of the sitter. Moreover, the warmish pinks and purples of the sofa covers – together with the browns of the table and floor – also play off against the cool colours of the subject's clothes. This contrast helps to focus attention on the sitter. In terms of colour, the picture is further lifted by the lively pattern of blues and yellows on her blouse.

Looking at shape

Understanding how shapes work together is a major part of painting. The woman's pose – half lying, half sitting – creates an interesting, fluid shape. This is set off against the angularly shaped expanses of the velvet throws. The coffee table in the foreground helps lead the eye into the picture.

▲ Note how most of the detailed work in the painting has been reserved for the sitter and her clothes. The rest of the painting has been completed in relatively loose washes.

FIRST STROKES

1 ▼ **Sketch in the scene** Using a 2B pencil and light but legible strokes, sketch the model and the draped sofa, checking the angles and proportions of the figure. Don't be afraid to erase parts of the drawing with a putty rubber and start again.

2 ▲ **Establish the backdrop** With a No. 10 round brush, block in the background throw with light washes of Winsor violet. Now take up a No. 6 round and work on some smaller areas. Begin on the face and hands with a very watery Naples yellow and the broad headband with burnt sienna. Throw the model's head forward by adding strong shadows in Winsor violet behind it.

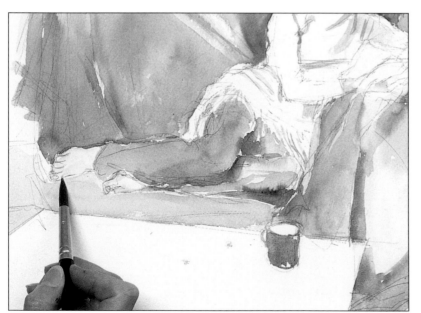

3 ▲ **Fill in the scene** With the No. 10 brush, paint the foreground fabric in purple madder alizarin, and deepen the background fabric with mixes of purple madder alizarin and Winsor violet, adding permanent rose highlights. With a wash of Payne's grey and a touch of French ultramarine, paint the trousers, the fringed shawl and the shadows on the blouse and wall. Use raw sienna over burnt sienna for the sofa, raw sienna on the sitter's headband, Naples yellow for the feet and French ultramarine for the mug.

DEVELOPING THE PICTURE

The main areas of your composition are now blocked in, and the pale and brighter colour registers are established. Progress by working with a range of other colours, right across the picture, using various paint thicknesses and techniques.

4 ▲ **Add upper-body detail** Changing to a No. 6 round brush, use the tip to pattern the blouse with watery raw sienna. Add a little more Payne's grey on the fringed shawl. Dot in the design on the headband in burnt umber and sepia.

5▲ **Brighten the blouse** Still using the pointed tip of the No. 6 brush, lift the whole scene by painting in the blue parts of the blouse pattern with cerulean blue.

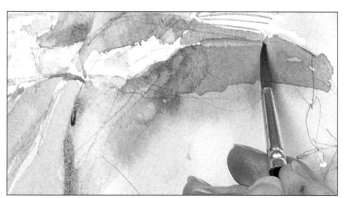

6▲ **Paint in the book** Now bring the model's book into the picture, balancing the right-hand side of the painting. Use the fine tip of the No. 6 brush to sketch in an outline of the book cover in watery sepia. Put in the faintest suggestion of the pages in the same colour. Working wet-in-wet, use sepia and Payne's grey to block in the book cover. With a mix of purple madder alizarin and Payne's grey, paint the shadow of the book on the throw.

7▲ **Work on the large areas** Taking up the No. 10 brush, start working up more depth and richness on the two throws. Use purple madder alizarin on both of them, laying thin washes over the dried colour to suggest the texture and sheen of velvet.

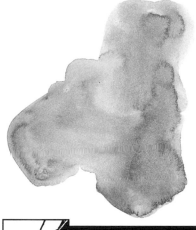

◄ Sepia (top), Winsor violet (bottom right) and purple madder alizarin (left) have been used extensively in the picture and help to set its overall colour key. They harmonize well with each other, creating an air of calm.

EXPERT ADVICE
Be complementary

By making use of complementary colours (opposites on the colour wheel) in a prominent part of the scene, you can really lift the whole. Here, placing brown-yellow and blue together in the blouse's pattern enhances the colours and brings a bright but balanced element to the picture.

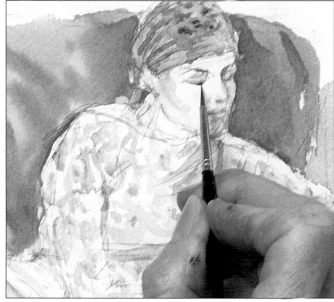

8▲ **Define the facial features** Now turn your attention to the face. With a No. 2 round, start to add some fine detailing with intense sepia paint. Wash a little watery burnt sienna over the lips.

9 ▾ Intensify the darks With the No. 10 and No. 6 brushes, use a mix of cerulean blue and black to define the feet and legs by adding shadows on and between them. Intensify the shadows across the blouse, too. Using the No. 10 brush, wash strong Naples yellow across the table as a base colour.

10 ▾ Work on some detail Use the same blue-black mix and the tip of the No. 6 brush to define the shawl's fringe, then dot ultramarine along its border. Mix up cerulean and emerald paints, and wash this across the wall behind the sofa. Notice how leaving the pencil underdrawing in has created some surface interest and definition.

Express yourself
A different viewpoint

This painting, also in watercolours, creates a different mood to the step-by-step one. The high viewpoint – combined with the curled, sleeping body position – provides a highly original figure study. Note how the model's nightgown is beautifully described by controlled wet-on-wet washes. The contrast in tone here – from the white of the paper to the deep blue shadow in the middle of her curl – really brings out the form of the body. The teapot and cup and saucer in the corner pick up on blue of the nightgown and help to balance the composition.

11 ▴ Adding definition With the No. 6 round, sweep lines of dry sepia, burnt umber and raw umber across the table to suggest wood grain. Using a 'palette mud' mix of black, burnt umber and ultramarine, strengthen the shadows on the legs and next to the mug. Add sepia to this mix to build up the tone of the book. Paint a little sepia and burnt sienna on the feet and hands, and a touch more detailing on the fringed border of the scarf.

A FEW STEPS FURTHER

Now that you have worked hard on bringing up the detail on the reclining figure, even up the balance of the picture by giving a little more attention to the larger expanses of plain colour on the throws and sofa seat.

12 ▶ **Finish the drapes** Wash some plain water across the throws to give them more drama and depth. Using Winsor violet and the No. 6 brush, strengthen the shadows on the background throw. Wash a little cadmium red lightly over the foreground throw.

13 ▲ **Bring up the sofa** Using the No. 10 round, add the final touch by washing watery sepia across the front of the sofa seat. Now the drapes, table and model are all well balanced, and the central figure retains its solidity, strength and interesting visual detail.

THE FINISHED PICTURE

A White highlights
The tiniest flecks of unpainted white paper are sufficient to represent white highlights on the luxurious fabric.

B Central interest
Attention to detail by painting the pattern on the fringed shawl brings a point of interest to the centre of the picture.

C Drawing the viewer in
The artist has placed a strongly coloured object – the mug – in the foreground to help draw the viewer into the picture.

Conservatory in watercolour

Watercolour is the ideal medium to use for the fresh colours in this conservatory scene. The sunlight streaming in creates strong diagonal shadows that offer a contrasting tonal element.

If you are lucky enough to own – or have access to – a conservatory, be sure to use it in a painting. Flooded with natural light, it provides a great subject – you not only have the plants and furniture inside to paint, but also the views of the world outside.

Balanced composition
The conservatory that our artist chose to paint has the added advantage of providing a simple, symmetrical composition. The bare floorboards in the foreground slant in from each side and extend into the distance, helping to create a sense of perspective and pulling the viewer's eye into the picture. The sofa balances the table in the middle of the composition, while the bushy plants on the shelf on the left are complemented by the spindly one in the hanging basket on the right-hand side.

The view outside
Beyond all this, we can see into the garden. As our artist painted in spring, the foliage is pale and golden. To capture the freshness of its colours, she found green-gold and lemon yellow particularly useful paints. These were applied unmixed for the sunlit areas of the garden, and with added touches of Payne's grey, cerulean and indigo for the shadow area.

If you are painting later, in the summer, you'll find that the greenery is darker in tone and cooler in colour. You'll need to increase the blue bias of your mixes to compensate for this.

▶ **The light tones in this painting were laid down first, then the darker areas were put in, some wet-on-wet and others wet-on-dry.**

A3 piece of watercolour paper

HB pencil

10 watercolours: ultramarine; Payne's grey; sepia; green-gold; lemon yellow; cerulean; indigo; alizarin crimson; yellow ochre; Prussian blue

Brushes: Nos. 3, 10 and 24 soft rounds

Watercolour palette or dish

Jar of water

Tissue or kitchen paper

FIRST STROKES

1 ▶ Sketch the scene
With the HB pencil, carefully draw the interior. The drawing should be relatively detailed. Correct any mistakes you make at this stage. When you move on to the watercolour, it will be too late!

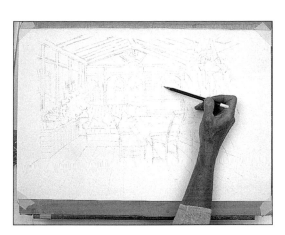

2 ◀ Establish the architecture
Using a mix of ultramarine, Payne's grey and sepia, draw the frame of the conservatory and trellis with a No. 3 round brush. To establish the right-hand shadow, let watery washes of all three colours run into each other.

DEVELOPING THE PICTURE

Having established the framework of the conservatory, move on to the garden. Don't worry about putting in too much detail here. Instead, look carefully at the variety of colours in the foliage – they range from inky blues to pale, golden yellows.

3 ▲ Move outside to the garden Switch to a No. 10 round brush to begin painting the garden. Use a mix of green-gold and lemon yellow to capture the effect of sunshine falling on the spring foliage.

4 ▲ **Add some darker tones** To put in the darker foliage, add cerulean and indigo to your mix of green-gold and lemon yellow. Keep varying the proportion of each colour in your mix to do justice to the variety of colours in the garden. Add sepia to your mix to render the woodwork outside.

5 ▲ **Continue the garden** For the wall outside, add alizarin crimson to the green-gold/lemon yellow mix. Add a little yellow ochre to a yellow mix to work the trees.

6 ▶ **Build up the pot plants** Apply a weak Payne's grey (with touches of the dark green mix) over the pot plants on the left. Create a range of greens by adding lemon yellow, green-gold and yellow ochre to indigo, cerulean and Payne's grey. Use these mixes to work up the leaves of the indoor plants with the No. 3 brush.

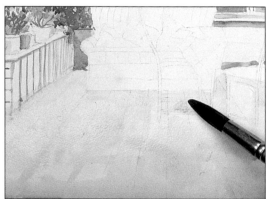

7 ▲ **Render the floor** Throw away your dirty water and replace it. Dip a No. 24 brush into the clean water and wet the bottom of the picture. Then add a wash of yellow ochre.

CONTROLLING RUNS

TROUBLESHOOTER

The beauty of working wet-on-wet is the element of chance as the washes run into unexpected places. However, if you need to, you can exercise some control by soaking up excessive paint with a tissue.

8 ▲ **Add alizarin crimson** While the floor wash is still wet, add some alizarin crimson to the immediate foreground. Then use the same colour on the No. 10 brush to paint the sofa and the plant pot on the left.

▲ Lemon yellow, Prussian blue and a touch of Payne's grey were some of the colours used to mix a range of grey-greens for the indoor plants.

9 ▲ **Lay the tablecloth** Use a wash of yellow ochre on the hanging basket in the top-right corner. Then apply a watery cerulean to the tablecloth. Surrounded by warm reds and yellows, this colour really stands out.

10 ▲ **Render the chairs** Use sepia with a little alizarin crimson to darken the underside of the hanging basket, then use the same mix to render the chairs and sofa cushions. Mix lemon yellow and yellow ochre for the pattern on the tablecloth.

11 ▲ **Darken the tone** Apply a wash of Prussian blue with touches of Payne's grey to darken the tone of the tablecloth. Also use this mix for the chair-seat covers.

Express yourself
A detailed rendering

This version of the painting is a much more detailed interpretation of the scene, both inside and outside the conservatory. The wall and fence in the garden are defined more precisely, as are the floorboards and checked pattern on the tablecloth.

Note also how the artist has used a deep-toned green for the foliage in the top-left corner. Like the wet-on-wet shadow at bottom left, this helps to direct the viewer's eye towards the garden in the centre of the composition.

12 ▼ **Add the hanging plant** Create a green with a mix of yellow ochre and cerulean to draw the plant in the hanging basket. Vary the colour and tone of the stalks as you work downwards.

13 ▲ **Finish the plant** Add a little indigo to your mix of yellow ochre and cerulean to put in more stalks of the hanging plant. For other stalks, use almost neat yellow ochre. Then, with the No. 24 brush, wet the paper at the bottom and loosely wash in Payne's grey with touches of Prussian blue for the shadows on the floor.

A FEW STEPS FURTHER

To complete the painting, intensify the shadow on the right to help draw the eye into the centre of the composition. Then simply refine a few of the details, including the chair legs and flowerpots.

14 ▶ **Strengthen the shadow** Still working with watery washes, reinforce the shadow tone on the right wall with Payne's grey and touches of alizarin crimson. Also re-establish the legs of the table and chairs if they have been altered by the wash put on the floor in the previous step.

15 ▲ **Add the finishing touches** Model the flower pots on the window ledge by adding darker tones with Payne's grey, sepia and alizarin crimson. Then put in some final details on the sofa's upholstery.

THE FINISHED PICTURE

A Muted shades
The leaves of the potted plants were rendered with a beautifully subtle range of blues, yellows and greens painted over a pale grey underwash.

B Warm colours
The glowing golden yellows of the foliage outside the conservatory help to pull the viewer's eye through the picture and into the garden.

C Wet-on-wet washes
Working wet-on-wet has created bold, dramatic shadows in the bottom right corner. These contrast with the light, airy tones at the top of the picture.

Chinese interior

A cool, calm interior with a view on to a sunlit exterior produces a striking pattern of lights and darks. Focus on these contrasts to create an image that lingers in the mind.

Interior views provide the artist with a fascinating and endlessly rewarding subject. In the project on the following pages, the artist has painted the interior of the Chen Family Temple in Guangzhou in China. Two photographs provide the reference for the project. The one on the right provided the composition's broad outlines and details such as the lattice-work shutters and the play of light across the space. From the left-hand picture, the artist borrowed the details of the bright red lanterns in the courtyard beyond.

Dark against light

This study focuses on a dark interior seen against a bright exterior. The near-silhouette, or *contre jour* image, simplifies the picture into areas of light, shade and cast shadow, emphasizing the abstract qualities in the subject. And where light falls through the lattice-work, it creates interesting and intricate patterns.

The success of a *contre jour* subject depends on achieving a pleasing balance of light and dark. With watercolour, it is important to work from light to dark because you can't paint light colours over dark ones without compromising the transparency of the medium. Start by applying

the sunny washes in the window openings. Work wet-on-wet with thin washes in these areas so that the paper shines through and creates a strong sense of luminosity. In the shaded areas, use wet-on-wet to give depth and vibrancy, but retain wet-on-dry for the areas where edges and decorative details are seen against the light.

▶ **The fine lattice-work of the window screen and the delicately carved legs of the plant stand create dark patterns against the sunlit exterior view.**

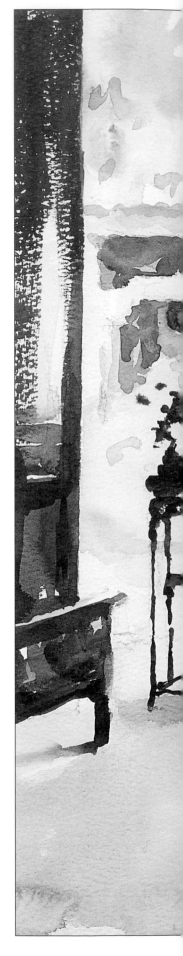

YOU WILL NEED	
Piece of 300gsm (140lb) NOT watercolour paper 40 x 30cm (16 x 12in)	chrome yellow; indigo; yellow ochre; cadmium red; alizarin crimson; ivory black
Soft carpenter's pencil	Brushes: Nos. 12 and 10 rounds
7 watercolours: cerulean blue;	Cotton bud Paper tissue

FIRST STROKES

1 ▼ Sketch the scene Use a soft carpenter's pencil to draw in the main outlines of the scene – the shutters framing the window openings, the angle of the floor and the low rail on the right. The flat-tipped carpenter's pencil gives a combination of thick and thin marks, so you can delineate edges and suggest areas of tone.

2 ▼ Establish the light Add a little cerulean blue to a chrome yellow wash to produce a pale greenish-yellow. Use a No. 12 round brush to wash in colour where the foliage is brightest. This underwash establishes the colour key for the sunlit courtyard.

3 ▶ Add more green
While the initial wash is still wet, drop touches of chrome yellow here and there. Add more of the greenish-yellow mixed in step 2 to suggest foliage outside the window. Mix indigo and yellow ochre for the darker greens and apply touches of unmixed chrome yellow. Allow the colours to bleed together. Use the brush tip to 'draw' the pot plant.

EXPERT ADVICE
Lifting wet colour

Introduce subtle textures and pale areas into the foliage by working into the still-wet wash with a cotton bud, absorbing some of the paint.

4 ◀ Introduce cool colours Mix a pale wash of indigo, cadmium red and alizarin crimson, and use this to block in the stonework of the buildings seen through the window. Use a darker wash of the same mix to depict the floor, the balcony and the shadows on the building across the courtyard.

6 ▲ Add the dark interior shadows The interior panelling is painted a deep blue-green that resonates against the sunny exterior. Mix indigo, alizarin crimson and a touch of chrome yellow. Load the No. 12 brush with the wash and drag it across the surface of the paper so that speckles of white show through here and there.

5 ◀ Dab out light areas Before the paint dries, estimate the position of the red lanterns in your composition. Then take a piece of paper tissue and begin to lift the still-wet wash in these areas.

8 ▼ **Develop the foreground** Block in the tables in the foreground with the indigo/alizarin crimson/chrome yellow mix. Half-close your eyes to simplify the areas of light and dark. Add ivory black and more indigo to the mix. Use the tip of a No. 10 round brush to put in the darkest shadows, which give form to the objects.

7 ▲ **Block in more darks** Continue painting the window screens and the pillar, using the brush to pick out details and leaving the white paper to stand for open areas and highlights. Add a little ivory black to the wash for the darkest areas.

DEVELOPING THE PICTURE

Now that the broad composition is established, you can start to add details, such as the graceful plant stands and the delicate tracery on the window screens. The trick is to provide enough information for the viewer to be able to 'read' the textures and details in the picture, without overworking or confusing the image. If every part of the painting is rendered with the same sharp detail it can be distracting, but if you add details at key points the eye will fill in the gaps.

9 ◄ **Add details** Load the No. 12 brush with the dark shadow mix and use the very tip of the brush to paint the delicate shapes of the plant stands. Work slowly and carefully, pulling and pushing the wash to create the solid forms of the table tops and drawing the brush very lightly down the paper for the graceful legs.

10 ► Add the tracery Add a touch of chrome yellow to an indigo wash and use this dark green to paint the plant on the stand. With the tip of the brush, suggest its delicate form seen against the light. Add a touch of alizarin crimson to the wash and, using the same No. 12 brush, suggest the delicate tracery on the window screens.

Express yourself
Sharp in black and white

The same balance of light and dark is retained in this pen-and-ink drawing of the Chinese interior, but the medium allows for more detail. The fine lines of the lattice-work are sharply defined, and the plant on the left is revealed as a bonsai tree.

11 ▼ Add foreground details Add black to the previous wash and use this to develop details on the furniture in the foreground. Use the tip of the brush to depict the narrow railing that divides the room.

A FEW STEPS FURTHER

The image now has a wonderful sense of light flooding into a shaded interior. While the balance of warm and cool colours is pleasing, a splash of colour contrast will enliven it and provide a focus for the eye.

12 ▲ Add the red lanterns Mix cadmium red and alizarin crimson for the lanterns. Blot with tissue, then draw the ribs on the lamp with the brush tip.

13 ▶ Adjust the screen Darken the shadows lying behind the lanterns with a mix of cerulean blue and indigo. Increase the brightness coming through the window screen by lightening the lower panel. Do this by dipping a cotton bud in water and lightly working it over the area to moisten it and lift some of the colour.

14 ▲ Add details Mix yellow ochre and indigo, and use this mossy green to paint the graceful leaves of the pot plant. Apply a pale wash of chrome yellow to add colour and detail to the foliage outside.

THE FINISHED PICTURE

A Creating recession
The details that are seen through the window are paler and less crisply defined than those found within the room, helping to create a convincing sense of depth.

B Coloured shadows
Cast shadows are rarely solid or black, but reflect colours from their surroundings. In this interior, the shadows pick up the blues from the panelling.

C Sparkling light
The dark paint used for the interior was dragged in bands across the textured paper, leaving white speckles of paper on either side to suggest sparkling light.

Moody church interior

Capture the magnificent interior of this church using a combination of watercolour and gouache.

This candlelit church presents the artist with a double challenge – how to portray accurately the impressive scale and detail of the building, while at the same time conveying a sense of drama and atmosphere.

As with any architectural subject, accuracy is essential. Begin by making a precise line drawing, establishing the perspective and including as many features as possible. Once you have drawn the subject correctly in pencil, you can then apply the colour freely and with confidence.

Watercolour and gouache

The artist first blocked in the dark and mid tones, applying watercolour washes with a large brush, to create the effect of flickering candlelight and contrasting dark shadows. The washes range from deep, cool purple to warm, earthy brown and are mixed from just three basic colours: black, indigo and burnt sienna.

If you have taken the time to make an accurate drawing, you can be much looser when painting. Let spontaneous runs and splashes form and don't worry about painting over the drawn lines. However, do make sure you leave plenty of unpainted paper between each area of colour to enhance the tonal contrast.

Gouache is reserved for the later stages as it is stronger and more opaque than watercolour. It is used to accentuate the dark shadows and to add local colour and highlights.

▼ Precise pencil drawing is combined with a loose painting style and strong tonal contrasts in this atmospheric interior.

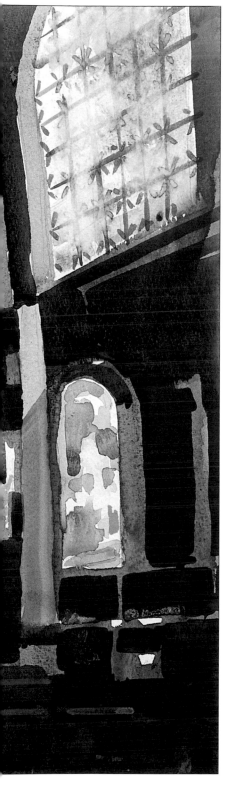

FIRST STEPS

1 ▼ **Start with a drawing** Make a detailed drawing of the subject, using a propelling pencil. Take great care to be accurate with the proportions and perspective.

2 ▼ **Block in the dark tones** Mix a wash of ivory black and indigo watercolour. Prop up the top of the board slightly, then start to block in the darkest areas of the vaulted ceiling, using a 25mm (1in) flat wash brush. Add a little water to the wash to vary the tones slightly.

3 ▼ **Add warm tones** Change to a No. 10 round brush and continue blocking in the dark tones. Add burnt sienna to the wash for the warmer areas, such as inside the arch behind the altar. Use the point of the bristles for detail and to paint around the candlesticks.

◄ **Golden tones are mixed from cadmium yellow (far left), burnt sienna (top) and orange gouache.**

4 ▲ **Continue blocking in** Returning to the flat wash brush, block in the remaining cool shadows with varying mixtures of black, indigo and burnt sienna. Work with short, vertical strokes to create the rectangular architectural shapes (see Expert Advice, below).

EXPERT ADVICE
Using a flat brush

The chisel-shaped bristles of a flat brush are ideal for painting sharp angles and geometric shapes. The rectangular shadows on the right side of the picture are blocked in quickly using controlled vertical strokes. The stairs are painted by dragging the brush sideways along each step.

6 ▼ Create mid tones Dilute the warm and cool washes further and block in mid tones, such as on the columns and the religious painting. Add cadmium red and cadmium yellow for warm tones behind the altar. Use paper tissue to absorb runs ofpaint and lighten the tones.

7 ▲ Add local colour Add more cadmium yellow and cadmium red to the warm wash from step 6 for local colour on the columns and altar. Mix cadmium yellow and yellow ochre for the candlelit recess on the right. With the wash brush, paint the windows in dilute ultramarine – use short, vertical strokes, allowing plenty of white paper to show through.

5 ▶ Use fluid strokes Using the same warm and cool mixes, depict the steps, rails, columns and the area behind the altar with the tip of the No. 10 round. Paint the frieze and the arch on the right as continuous strokes of colour. Leave to dry.

DEVELOPING THE PICTURE

Put aside the watercolours and continue the painting using opaque gouache colours to accentuate the deepest shadows, including the vaulted ceiling.

8 ▼ Introduce gouache Working with the No. 10 round brush, strengthen the shadows on the left with a deep purple mixed from ultramarine and orange gouache. Use the brush tip to paint around the altar drapes and carved stonework.

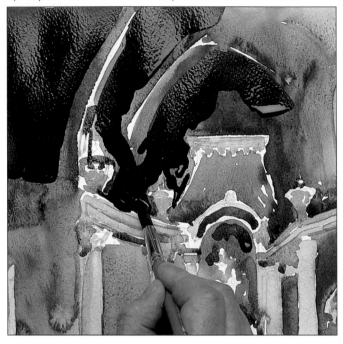

9 ▲ Develop the shadows Dilute the mixture and add a little more orange to paint the shadows in the altar drapes and on the right-hand arches.

EXPERT ADVICE
Paint straight lines

Ruled lines of paint give stonework in buildings a realistic appearance – but you only need a few. Too many straight lines will make the image look flat and mechanical. Use a ruler to help you pick out some of the fluting on the columns, holding the edge of the ruler above the paper surface in order to avoid smudging.

10 ▲ Add fine detail For the finer shading, change to a No. 4 round brush and use the tip to paint around the candlesticks. Depict carving on the cornice and columns, and paint the rails. Define the column on the left of the altar with a mix of burnt sienna and ultramarine (see Expert Advice, left).

11 ▼ **Paint the recess** Paint the candlelit recess with mixes of orange, cadmium yellow and burnt sienna gouache, toned down with ultramarine. Add a shadow to the right-hand pillar with a well-diluted mix of ultramarine and orange.

Express yourself
Capturing the atmosphere

Try painting the church without first making a detailed drawing. This version is done in watercolour and oil pastel and is a quarter of the size of the main painting. The small scale and chunky pastel sticks emphasize colour and atmosphere, rather than architectural details.

A FEW STEPS FURTHER

The golden ornaments and light reflections are focal points of the painting and must show up clearly against the surrounding darkness. Use pure white gouache, or white mixed with cadmium yellow and orange.

12 ▲ **Introduce white gouache** Paint the fluting at the top of the columns, using titanium white gouache and a No. 2 round brush. Mix the white with a little cadmium yellow for the candlesticks and ornaments, leaving flecks of unpainted paper to represent the reflections and highlights.

13 ▲ **Develop the columns** Model the candlesticks by adding orange to the mix. Use a ruler and the tip of the brush to pick out some of the fluted shadows in a mix of orange and ivory black. Blend the fluted lines at the base of the column to create solid shadow.

14 ▼ **Paint the window panes** With the help of a ruler, use the tip of the No. 2 brush to paint the leading on the large window in a dilute mix of black and indigo gouache.

15 ▲ **Lighten the window** Finally, use a small, damp sponge to soften the leading and give the impression of sunlight streaming through the window panes.

THE FINISHED PICTURE

A Cool lighting
The cool, blue daylight seen through the arched windows contrasts effectively with the warm glow of the interior candlelight.

B Offset composition
To avoid a symmetrical painting, the altar is deliberately offset to the left of the composition.

C Focal colour
The strongest colour in the painting is the bright orange gouache used on the easel in the centre of the composition. The eye is immediately attracted to this and the other areas of warm colour.

Going underground

Most of the time, travelling on crowded trains might seem a bit of a chore. But remember, there's a potential painting in every carriage and on every platform.

Although painting from real life has much to commend it, there are occasions when working from a photographic reference is useful, and sometimes essential. This step-by-step is a good example. The scene at a London Underground station would be almost impossible to render working from real life. Instead, the artist has photographed it and painted it later in the comfort of his home. Remember, a compact camera can fit into a pocket or handbag and – if used with an eye for the potential of everyday situations – can provide a wealth of painting material.

A painterly subject

In choosing what to photograph, the artist's eye for colour and composition led him to focus on a man sitting alone on his suitcase, oblivious to all around him. The subject is naturally framed by the wall on the left, and by the rail tracks on the top right-hand side. The colours in the photo also work well – the red of the jacket immediately throws the subject to the fore, while the muted clothes of the other figures help them to recede.

When it came to translating the photo into a painting, the artist tweaked colours and details. The figures and objects surrounding the seated man were reduced to simple planes of colour and restricted to a palette of blues and greens in order to emphasize the solitary figure in his red jacket.

▲ Dabbing cotton wool on damp washes of paint has helped to create the wonderful array of textures, tones and edges in this picture of a traveller on the London Underground.

FIRST STROKES

1 ▼ **Sketch the main outline** Using the photo as a guide, sketch the image with a 4B pencil. The key elements to capture are the strong diagonal lines of the rail tracks in the top right-hand corner, the seated man in the foreground and the outlines of the figures behind him.

2 ▼ **Block in the clothes** Mix a dilute wash of cadmium scarlet and ultramarine; apply to the jacket, using a No. 6 brush. Mix Prussian blue and cadmium yellow pale to paint the bag next to the face of the seated figure. Using dilute yellow ochre, wash the jacketed figure at upper left. Add a little Prussian blue to the wash to make a green for the trousers of the figure on the right. Now mix Prussian blue and Payne's grey, and paint the trousers of the seated figure. Dilute the wash and apply to the figure's shoe.

EXPERT ADVICE
Special effects

To achieve areas of lighter tone just after you have applied a watercolour wash, gently rub out sections of paint with a small piece of damp cotton wool. Here, a pale patch has been lifted from the seat of the dark blue trousers, and another area is being removed from the green trousers.

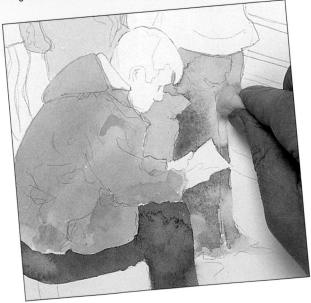

3 ▼ Continue blocking in Mix yellow ochre, cadmium yellow pale and a dot of Prussian blue; paint the undefined figure on the left. Mix ultramarine and Prussian blue and wash the jacket of the figure on the right. To this mix, add cadmium scarlet, yellow ochre, and a little more ultramarine to creaate a black-brown for the suitcase. Use a dilute wash of ultramarine to fill in the small area behind the seated figure.

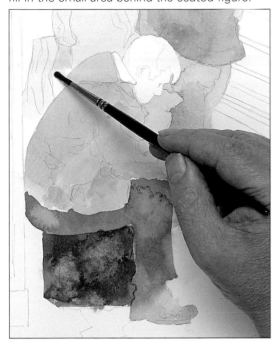

4 ▶ Paint the platform Mix yellow ochre and cadmium yellow to 'draw' the line on the platform. Add cadmium scarlet to make a skin tone for the face. Mix indigo, ultramarine and yellow ochre; paint the tracks, using a No. 8 brush. Wash dilute cadmium yellow pale, Prussian blue and ultramarine over the platform, and dilute ultramarine on the wall. Mix cadmium red light and Payne's grey for the background.

5 ▶ Add tracks Using a No. 4 brush, apply a yellow ochre/ultramarine wash to the back of the hair. Then paint the tracks with the blue trouser mix and allow to dry. Wash yellow ochre across the tracks. Add ultramarine and Payne's grey and define their contours.

6 ▼ Silhouette head and hands Define the hood with Payne's grey. Make an ultramarine/yellow ochre mix and wash over the jacket at upper left. Mix indigo and yellow ochre to darken the green trousers, adding small dabs of pure yellow ochre and indigo while the paint is still wet.

7 ◀ Build up tone Mix Payne's grey and ultramarine, and, using the No. 6 brush, apply this to the dark blue trousers. Leave the knee section lighter, and rub back the whole area with damp cotton wool. Mix ultramarine and cadmium yellow pale and wash over the platform with the No. 8 brush. Squeeze damp cotton wool so that a few drops of water fall on to this area and rub gently to give a mottled effect to the paint surface.

DEVELOPING THE PICTURE

The basic areas of colour are now blocked in and it is time to develop the forms with tonal shading. Continue using damp cotton wool or a cotton bud to rub back any hard edges.

8▲ **Add texture to the platform** Returning to the No. 6 brush, overlay a wash of ultramarine and Payne's grey on the platform area in the bottom left-hand corner.

9▲ **Build up tone** With a cadmium scarlet/yellow ochre mix, vary the tone on the red jacket. Define areas of the green trousers with indigo and cadmium yellow pale. Mix cadmium yellow, scarlet, yellow ochre and cadmium yellow pale; paint the hands. Now mix indigo, carmine, cadmium red light and yellow ochre, and apply to the suitcase. Wash an ultramarine/yellow ochre/Prussian blue mix over the blue jacket and bag.

10▶ **Add detail** Return to the jacket, mixing Payne's grey and cadmium scarlet and dotting under the arm with the No. 4 brush. Use the brush to smudge the colour from under the arm to the edge of the jacket. Draw a curve at the side of the jacket to indicate a fold line.

11 ▶ **Add features** Use cotton wool to smudge any hard red edges. Mix yellow ochre, cadmium scarlet and a little ultramarine. With a No. 2 brush, define the ear, nose, forehead and cheek. Rub back the cheek with a damp cotton bud. Apply a mix of yellow ochre and ultramarine to the hair.

▼ **Cadmium scarlet/yellow ochre (left) and cadmium scarlet/ultramarine (right) are the two basic mixes used for the red jacket.**

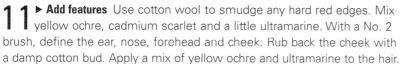

12 ▶ **Vary tones** Mix cadmium yellow, ultramarine and cadmium scarlet, then wash along the platform edge with the No. 8 brush. Darken the rails with a Payne's grey/ultramarine mix.

Express yourself
Single or return?

Another familiar scene at an Underground station, this composition is full of graphic linear elements, such as the ticket-office window, the noticeboard and the bands on the wall.

A FEW STEPS FURTHER

Finish off the picture by working some additional surface interest to give the painting character.

13 ▲ **Add foreground interest** Mix indigo and aureolin, and wash over the platform area. Flick a few drops of water on to the wet paint. Allow to dry, and wash roughly over the top with dilute cadmium yellow, using the No. 8 brush. Rub back with a piece of damp cotton wool.

14 ▲ **Spotting and dribbling** Using the No. 4 brush, apply dilute washes of cadmium yellow, cadmium red light and ultramarine to the wall. Using the No. 2 brush, draw an ultramarine border on the wall and platform. To create a lively picture surface, dribble a line of cadmium yellow pale on the left, then add dots and lines of cadmium red light.

THE FINISHED PICTURE

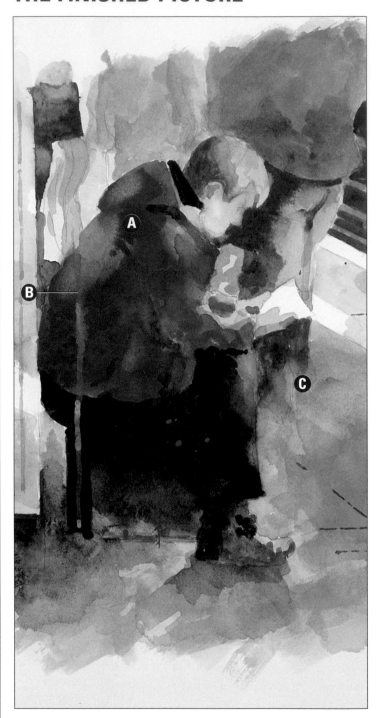

A Textured paint
The red jacket is the focus of the painting. It has been given a deep, textured appearance through the layering of colour and rubbing back of the paint with pieces of damp cotton wool.

B Distressed finish
By purposefully adding dribbles and spots of brightly coloured paint to the darker areas of the finished composition, the artist has given the painting a lift and a feeling of immediacy.

C Abstract shapes
The washes of colour around the central seated figure have been intentionally kept loose and abstract. They are represented as blocks of toned-down colour with little detail.

Sunlit interior

A soft pencil and a selection of warm colours recreate the comfortable atmosphere of this spacious, sunny sitting room.

Pencil and paint are perfect partners in this composition of a stylish interior. The artist began with a light pencil drawing to establish the composition, then painted in the main areas of colour quite loosely before drawing more tightly over the top.

Emphatic lines

The pencil used was a very dark, soft 8B, which is ideal for emphatic lines and deep, rich shading. It shows up well over the painted areas and so can be used to add details and textures once all the paintwork is complete.

Mix and match

A combination of watercolour and gouache was used to bring colour into the drawing, sunny yellow and an orange shades were used. Watercolour and gouache can be mixed together if necessary as they are both

▲ Soft pencil, gouache and watercolour complement each other beautifully in this line-and-wash drawing.

water-based paints, which is handy if you don't have all the colours you need in one or other of the mediums.

In hot weather or a warm room, gouache will dry out more quickly on the palette than watercolour, so spray the paint with water from a plant mister from time to time to keep it moist.

Piece of 300gsm (140lb) hot-pressed watercolour paper 46 x 61cm (16 x 24in)

8B pencil

Putty rubber (to erase mistakes and guide lines)

Craft knife (for sharpening pencil)

Brushes: No. 2 squirrel; No. 4 round

4 gouache paints: mid orange; cadmium yellow; titanium white; brilliant green

6 watercolours: brilliant purple; burnt umber; cobalt blue; gamboge; ultramarine violet; Payne's grey

Mixing palette or dish

Jar of water

SETTING THE SCENE

Before you embark on the project, make a rough, preliminary sketch to check the composition and work out the perspective of the furniture and other features in the room. The very free interpretation shown on the right is worked in the style of an interior designer's colour notes and is a great way to try out the paint mixes.

FIRST STEPS

1 ▶ Make an initial drawing Using an 8B pencil, draw the composition quite loosely. First establish the eye-level line – it runs just below the wall plaque. Make sure that the perspective lines of the sofa, rug and window frame meet at a vanishing point on this line.

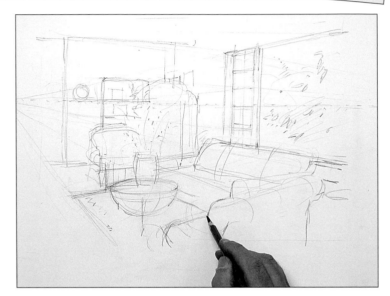

2 ▼ Colour the walls Mix mid orange and cadmium yellow gouache with titanium white to make an apricot colour. Using a No. 2 squirrel brush, wash this colour over the walls.

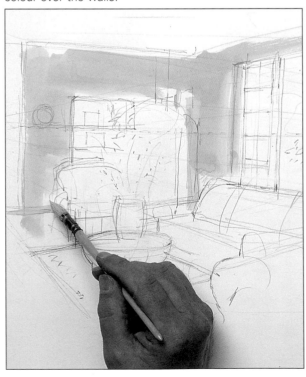

3 ▲ Paint the chairs and sofa Add more mid orange and water to the mix and wash over the armchairs. Now mix mid orange and a little white gouache with brilliant purple watercolour and paint the sofa and back of the foreground chair with this warm pink. Add more mid orange to the mix to make a 'burnt' orange for the far chair.

4 ▼ Mix in more colours Use the 'burnt' orange mix to block in the rug. Add brilliant green gouache to the warm pink mix from step 3 and paint the red plant. Mix in burnt umber watercolour to make a dark pinkish-brown for the shelf and floor shadows.

5 ▼ Put in the greens With the pinkish-brown mix, paint the back of the near armchair, the ceiling beam and the band around the table. Make a dilute mix of cobalt blue and gamboge watercolour for the hazy colour outside the window. For the plants, add brilliant green gouache to the apricot mix from step 2. Add extra cadmium yellow to vary the green.

DEVELOPING THE PENCIL WORK

Once you have finished washing in the colours, you can continue with the drawing. Emphasize the furniture with pencil outlines and put in pattern details on the rug and upholstery, working on top of the coloured areas.

6 ▲ Draw some details Using a No. 4 round brush and a mix of ultramarine violet watercolour and white gouache, paint the window frame. Sharpen the 8B pencil and define some of the leaves on the red plant. Begin outlining the furniture and hatch shadows on the floor around the far chair.

7 ▲ Put in some more detail Add more leaf detail to the red plant and darken the shadow areas within it. Work around the sofa cushions. Firm up the outline of the table, then draw the lines on the vase and hatch in its cast shadow. Draw the pattern on the rug, emphasizing the black edge.

8 ▲ **Continue with the pencil** Describe the plant next to the sofa with outlined leaves and dark negative shapes. Hatch in the shadow on the shelves. Indicate the curved back and arms of the chair in the foreground with linear marks.

9 ▲ **Use more colour** With the No. 4 round brush, dab on spots of titanium white gouache to suggest the flowers in the vase. Paint white highlights on the armchair, sofa and plants. Mix mid orange, cadmium yellow and white and suggest the pattern on the chairs and rug with simple brush marks. Develop the pattern using the warm pink mix from step 3. Use the pink mix on the red plant, too.

A FEW STEPS FURTHER

Take a look at the picture and check whether any textures would benefit from being described in more detail. For example, the leather sofa has a mottled appearance that can be suggested with a combination of pencil and paint.

EXPERT ADVICE
Gouache highlights

As white gouache is opaque rather than translucent like watercolour, it is ideal for adding strong highlights at the end of the project. Here, titanium white is being painted over the rich pink of the sofa to create a light area.

10 ▲ **Paint dark leaves on the plants** Mix a dark green from brilliant green gouache with brilliant purple and a little Payne's grey watercolour. Use this to paint individual leaves on the large green plant. On the red plant, use the dark green to pick out a few of the leaves and also to paint dark negative shapes behind paler leaves. Finally, rub out the pencil construction lines around the drawing.

11 ▼ **Add pencil and paint details** Using the 8B pencil, add more definition to the rug pattern. Mix mid orange and cadmium yellow gouache to paint the lines on the vase. Use the pinkish-brown mix for the round table frame, then add white gouache to the mix for the pale shadows on the table.

12 ▲ **Describe the leather texture** Use pencil hatching for the dark tone behind the armchair and to add texture to the leather sofa. Bring out the paler parts of the leather with the orange/yellow vase mix plus white.

THE FINISHED PICTURE

A Hazy background
The garden, just visible through the window, was left hazy, so that it did not distract from the interior.

B Loose paint style
The paintwork was kept loose, working with the drawn elements, rather than dominating them.

C Pencil over paint
Drawing back over the paint adds weight to the linear aspect of the drawing and builds up shadow tone.

The summer house

This conservatory interior has the delicacy of a tinted etching, but it was drawn with ordinary ballpoint pens. The 'tinting' was done in watercolour.

Ballpoint pens might not be the obvious choice of tools when making a drawing for a watercolour painting, but they provide an unusual, detailed effect that is very successful. The pen marks do not run, so you can apply washes of watercolour over the lines without spoiling the drawing or smudging the colour.

Regular line work

Lines can be made lighter or darker by varying the pressure as you draw. What you can't do with a ballpoint pen is vary the thickness of the line itself. The pen tends to suit small- and medium-sized drawings, as the pen lines can appear overly fine and insubstantial in larger pictures. This painting of a conservatory is worked at quite a small scale, so the pen lines look firm and decisive.

You must draw 'positively' with ball-point for your picture to be successful. Once a mark has been made it cannot easily be erased, so there is little room for error. To achieve a lively yet accurate ballpoint drawing, it is a good idea to start with a very light, preliminary pencil drawing. Once this is established to your satisfaction, the overdrawn ball-point lines can be as bold and spontaneous as you like.

Coloured outlines

This painting was executed from inside a conservatory, taking in a view of the garden beyond. The colours indoors were predominantly warm and cheerful, while outside the light was brighter and cooler. To capture this effect in the painting, the watercolour mixtures for the garden contained slightly more blue than those used in the conservatory. To emphasize the difference, the artist chose a black ballpoint for drawing the interior, while the garden was worked with a blue ballpoint.

In the final stages of the work, brightly coloured felt-tip pens were used to pick out some of the interior local colours and to highlight the ivy on the garden wall outside.

▲ **There is plenty to engage the viewer both inside and outside. The eye moves naturally from the room to the garden.**

▼ YOU WILL NEED	
Piece of stretched cartridge paper 30 x 40cm (12 x 16in)	Mixing palette or dish
HB pencil	10 watercolours: viridian; ultramarine; raw umber; cerulean; burnt umber; raw sienna; lemon yellow; yellow ochre; burnt sienna; cadmium red
2 ballpoint pens: black; blue	
Liquid paper for corrections	
No. 8 round brush	4 felt-tip pens: yellow; blue; red; grey

FIRST STROKES

1 ▼ **Draw the outline** Using an HB pencil, sketch in the position of the window, table and other main elements in the composition.

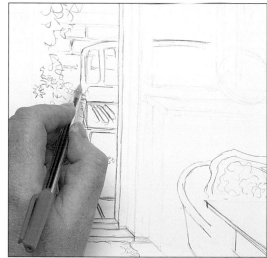

2 ◄ **Begin using ballpoint pens** Now start to work over the pencil lines with ballpoint pens, using black for the interior of the conservatory and blue for the garden visible through the door and window. Establish the main shapes with strong, clear lines.

3 ▼ Vary the lines Continuing with ballpoint pen, complete the drawing. Use light, broken lines in blue for the bricks and foliage seen through the window. For the ornaments and objects inside the conservatory, work in heavier, black lines.

4 ▼ Suggest tones Look for the darkest tones in the subject and indicate these with hatched and cross-hatched lines. These patches of tone will show through subsequent watercolour to represent pronounced areas of deep shadow.

DEVELOPING THE PICTURE

The drawing is done and it is now time to add colour. Don't worry if you feel the drawing might need a little more work. Ballpoint pen can be used over watercolour, so you can always go back and do more drawing when the paint is dry.

5 ▶ Introduce colour Mix a dilute watercolour wash of viridian with a touch of ultramarine. Using a No. 8 round brush, apply this loosely to the plant in the tub and the ivy on the garden wall. Allow some of the green to overlap on to the bricked area.

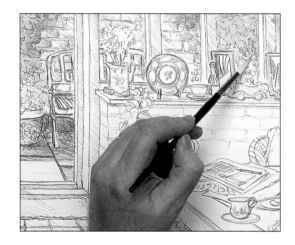

6 ▲ Paint the exterior Mix raw umber with a little cerulean and block in the shadow under the garden chair, allowing the cross-hatched ballpoint lines to show through. Apply the same mix to the brickwork on the garden wall.

Express yourself
Garden in bloom

Painting a smaller section of the same subject has allowed the artist to concentrate on the relationship between the exterior and interior. The red of the pot plant outside picks up on the cut flowers on the shelf. The cool blues of the climbing plant are repeated in the colours of the crockery. To suggest the presence of glass panes, the colours viewed through the window are pale and washy. Note, for instance, how the garden wall is described with well-defined, strong washes on the left of the picture, while pale mixes and lots of exposed white paper predominate in the middle section.

7 ▼ Develop the garden Block in the paved terrace in burnt umber with touches of raw sienna and cerulean. Paint the bench with a mix of viridian and ultramarine. Using a stronger mix of the same colour, dot in a few dark green shadows on the underside of the ivy leaves.

8 ▼ Start the interior Paint the shaded areas on the door and window frames in dilute raw umber mixed with a little lemon yellow. Use the same colour for the interior brickwork. Add a little viridian to the mixture and block in the two wicker chairs. Paint the table in yellow ochre.

9 ▲ Develop the interior Paint the tiles in a weak mix of burnt sienna and yellow ochre. Add the floor shadow, mat, floor joins, step and plant pot in varying mixes of yellow ochre and raw umber. Paint the cushion pattern in burnt sienna and cadmium red, and the plant, cushion and chair detail with a mix of viridian and ultramarine.

▶ **Mixes used in the interior include cerulean with burnt sienna (top) for the ornaments; viridian, lemon yellow and raw umber (centre) for the chairs; burnt sienna and yellow ochre (bottom) for the tiles.**

MAKING CORRECTIONS

TROUBLESHOOTER

Mistakes made with a ballpoint pen cannot be rubbed out, but you can correct them with a small amount of liquid paper. Note that watercolour applied over liquid paper is often paler than normal, so keep any corrections as small as possible.

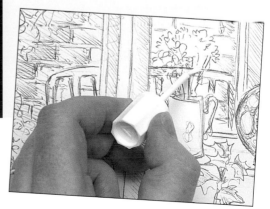

A FEW STEPS FURTHER

A few details and one or two splashes of colour and the interior will be complete. In these final stages, introduce brightly coloured felt-tip pens to sharpen the colours.

10 ▲ Define the ornaments Paint the shadows on the wooden window sill in raw sienna and raw umber. Use the tip of the brush to define the china jug and plate in cerulean with a touch of raw sienna. Paint the bottle, plant and remaining ornaments in the same colour mixed with viridian. Add ultramarine shadows to the plant.

11 ▲ Add more detail Define the outlines of the ornaments in burnt sienna and ultramarine. Paint the second chair and cushion in viridian with touches of ultramarine and burnt sienna. Moving to the objects on the table, paint the crockery and newspaper in lemon and cerulean with a touch of burnt sienna. Add the cup pattern and the shadow on the newspaper in a mixture of burnt sienna and viridian. Blot excess paint from the newspaper to lighten the tones.

12 ▶ Paint the teapot Complete the tableware, including the teapot, which is painted in burnt umber and viridian with cadmium red decoration.

13 ▼ **Add dark tones** Using the tip of the brush, define the wickerwork on the second chair in viridian and paint the red flowers on the cushion. Depict the newspaper text and crossword in a greyish mixture of ultramarine and burnt umber. Add shadows to the table top in raw umber and yellow ochre.

14 ▲ **Introduce felt-tips** Use felt-tip pens for some final splashes of strong tone and colour. Use yellow on the outdoor foliage, blue on the garden seat, and red on the cushion pattern. With a grey felt-tip pen, outline the newspaper, chairs and cushions.

THE FINISHED PICTURE

A Ballpoint pen effects
The original lines made with ballpoint pen show through the paint to give fine detail in some areas and dark tone in others.

B Defining shadows
Fine lines of shadow applied with grey felt-tip pen define the newspaper and other objects on the table.

C Linear perspective
The converging lines of the table and floor tiles lead the viewer's eye through the open door into the garden beyond.

Boatyard

The jumble of boatyard paraphernalia and splashes of bright colour keep your eye on the move around this watercolour painting.

This study was inspired by one of the artist's favourite haunts, his local boatyard in Cornwall. What captured his imagination was the array of textures and patterns. In the densely packed yard are tools of all shapes, sizes and textures. There are the undulations of the corrugated iron walls and a jumble

▼ **Elements from two photographs were combined to develop this composition, which is packed with detail.**

of ropes dangling from the ceiling. The result is a tapestry of random shapes, in which even the figures of the men at work are just part of the overall design.

Working on gesso

The artist decided to work on a textured surface to heighten these effects within the painting. He covered the line board used by graphic designers – available at art shops – with acrylic gesso. Painting on a gesso ground involves a different

approach to traditional watercolour techniques. The gesso seals the board, so that the paint floats on the surface rather than sinking into the support, creating interesting pools when it dries. The paint takes longer to dry and you have to work carefully when building up layers, as the original colour tends to lift off the surface. Be prepared for some happy accidents, but don't worry about mistakes – you can alter areas when they have dried.

YOU WILL NEED

Line board 34 x 46cm (13½ x 18in) primed with white acrylic gesso

4H pencil

12 watercolours: cerulean blue; ivory black; chrome yellow; phthalo blue; vermilion; magenta; Payne's grey; raw sienna; ultramarine; burnt sienna;

phthalo green; raw umber

Brushes: Small and large squirrel brushes; No. 3 sable round

Mixing palette or dish

Putty rubber

Steel ruler

FIRST STEPS

1 ▼ **Scale up the scene** Prime your line board with acrylic gesso and let it dry. Using a well-sharpened 4H pencil, copy the scene on to the board, including as much detail as you can. As it is an intricate drawing, it's best to copy the grid below, shown in light blue, on to your support – that is, with a ruler lightly pencil in eight equally spaced lines down the support and five equally spaced lines across it. This means you will be able to execture the drawing accurately, square by square.

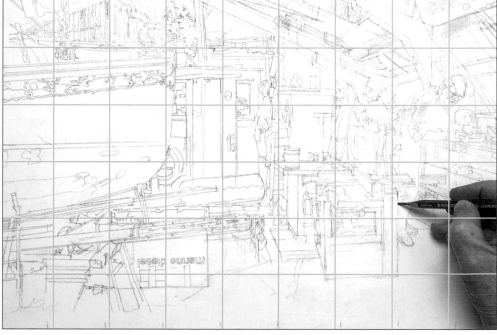

2 ▼ **Begin with a blue** Dilute some cerulean blue watercolour and, using a small squirrel brush, apply it along the rubbed-down paintwork on the boat. Then move on to other areas of blue. Add a little ivory black to the cerulean wash and make a subtle blue-grey to apply over the pale grey areas, such as details around the roof, workbench and on the window frame. When dry, feel free to use a putty rubber to soften the drawing so that it doesn't interfere with the painting.

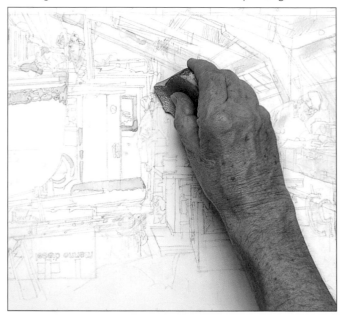

3 ▲ **Test your colours** Using the small squirrel brush and a dilute mix of chrome yellow, fill in the pale band along the hull and leave it to dry. Make a strong phthalo blue and try it out at the edge of the gesso board – testing colours is important when working on gesso, because it is difficult to modify them once they are down. Then use a large squirrel brush to apply this colour over the top half of the hull.

4 ▼ **Work wet-on-wet** Paint the base of the hull in a red mix of vermilion with a touch of magenta, working carefully around the drawn details. While the paint is still wet, drop some Payne's grey into it to suggest staining on the boat.

5 ▲ **Work around the board** Paint the overalls and oil drum in phthalo blue. Use the red mix to add bright details, modifying it with raw sienna and black where you need an orange tone, and ultramarine where you want a bluer effect. Now mix a very dilute brown from chrome yellow, phthalo blue and a hint of vermilion and wash this over the floor.

DEVELOPING THE PICTURE

Continue working up all the browns in the scene, varying their tones by making the mixes progressively stronger and darker.

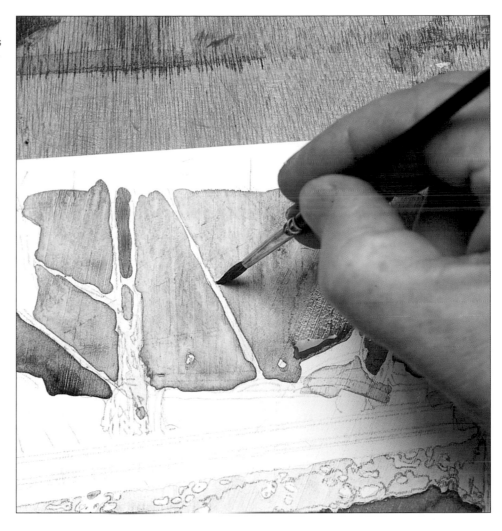

6 ▶ Start on the background Mix a mid brown from raw sienna, burnt sienna and chrome yellow. Using a No. 3 round sable brush, paint the background, taking care to avoid the various ropes and other items that cut across the area.

7 ▲ Add more browns Still working with the mix from step 6, paint other mid brown areas, such as the planks and door. Strengthen the tone and paint the box in the foreground. Then mix a dark brown from raw sienna, black and vermilion, and use the various brown mixes to paint lines along the top of the hull. Apply the dark brown to the door frame and behind the lifebelt.

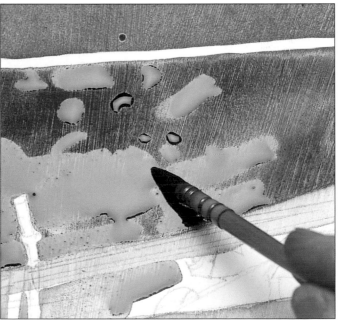

8 ▲ Suggest weathering on the hull To represent the weather beaten appearance of the hull, apply a watery mix of magenta and Payne's grey with the large squirrel brush. Work carefully – if you paint the new colour on too roughly, it will lift off the colour underneath.

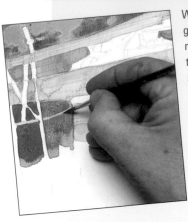

EXPERT ADVICE
Taking colour off

When working on gesso, it is easy to remove colour because the paint sits on the surface of the board rather than sinking into it. Here, the artist is using the tip of a brush dipped in clean water to take some blue off the top of the oil drum and suggest its metal lip.

9 ▶ Bring in some green
Using the small squirrel brush, paint the workman's jumper in ultramarine. Then mix a little black and raw sienna into phthalo green to make the muddy brown hues around the doorway. Overpaint some areas with black. Use phthalo green plus varying amounts of raw sienna and water for the small workbench in front of the figures – paint it wet-on-wet so that the colours pool together.

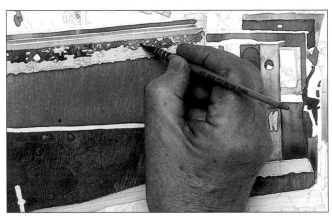

10 ▲ Add detail to the hull Paint a darker shade of blue over the weathered band on the boat's hull with a mix of cerulean blue and a little Payne's grey. Take care to avoid the pale patches as before.

11 ▶ Darken the man's overalls
Now give the men's clothes some texture. Using your original drawing to guide you, paint a layer of phthalo blue over the areas of the workman's overalls which are in shadow. Once the paint has dried, the texture of the board shows through, giving the appearance of tough denim fabric.

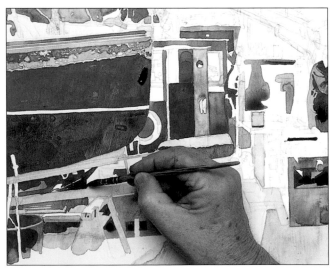

12 ▲ Paint under the boat Dilute the green mixes from step 10 and paint the trestle and other green details. Add shadows under the hull with a mix of black and varying amounts of ultramarine. It isn't necessary to know what every shape represents – just create a pleasing rhythm of patterns.

13 ▲ Add flesh tones Work up shadows on the right-hand man's clothes with mixes of phthalo blue or ultramarine and black. Paint pale skin tones on the faces with a watery mix of vermilion and raw sienna. Leave to dry, then use a stronger mix for the darker tones. Paint his beard with dilute raw umber.

14 ▼ **Fill in the background** Finish the figure in the foreground, painting his arms with the same light and dark skin tones as on his face. Now mix shades of grey from varying strengths of black plus phthalo blue and define the man's cap, glasses and watch strap. Then, with a more dilute mix of grey, add areas of shadow to the structure above his head.

15 ▼ **Paint the cocker spaniel** Define the horizontal mast with bands of dilute Payne's grey and burnt sienna. Then paint the spaniel. Use Payne's grey for the shadows on his coat, burnt sienna on his face and ears, and black for his nose, eyes and the tip of his ear. Leave the surface of the board for the white of his fur.

Express yourself

Setting up a scene

Monochrome sketches are a good way of working out the elements of a painting – the light and dark tones, the perspective and the most successful composition. In this charcoal sketch, the artist tried combining elements from his photos – putting in the two figures from one and the workbench and tea chest from the other – to see whether they held together. Without the colour, the drawing presents a more sombre view of the subject matter.

16 ▲ **Add the final details** Paint the skylights above the workbench with a mix of Payne's grey and raw umber. Mark in the tools and shadows on and around the workbenches with dilute Payne's grey, black, phthalo blue and a raw sienna/burnt sienna mix. Now, for one of the final patterns, paint the triangle of beams in the top left of the composition with the sienna mix.

A FEW STEPS FURTHER

There are a few more details that need to be brought into the painting to finish it off. For example, the lettering on the tea chest adds an authentic touch.

17 ▶ **Add dark details** Using the small squirrel brush and Payne's grey, work up a few dark patches of shadow in the clutter under the sloping roof. This helps to accentuate the element of pattern within the painting.

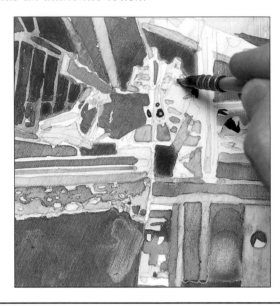

18 ▲ **Add lettering** Wash a cast shadow below the tea chest with a Payne's grey/burnt sienna mix, then touch in alizarin crimson on the labels. Finally, pick out the lettering with the tip of the brush.

THE FINISHED PICTURE

A Textured surface
The painted gesso ground works to heighten the sense of texture on the side of the boat and on the tea chest. Note how white ridges show through.

B Blocks of tone
The workmen, in their bold blue overalls, act as focal points in the yard's clutter. The masts in the foreground and the sloping roof help guide the eye to the men.

C Pools of colour
The tidemarks on the floor – painted wet-on-wet – add to the range and variety of textures. They work well against the geometric shapes elsewhere in the picture.

Train station

Lively pencil lines and loose washes of watercolour combine to create the distinctive appearance and atmosphere of a traditional railway terminus.

In this project, the artist has combined two photographs of a train station taken at slightly different angles. He wanted to include elements from both – the train plus the sweep of the platform on the right. The idea was to create an atmospheric rather than a realistic view: all the main elements are in place, but much of the detail, particularly the colours, is left to the imagination.

Inexperienced artists often believe that the more paints they use and the more brushes in their armoury, the better their paintings. This is rarely the case. More likely to be true is the maxim 'less is more'. This painting was, in fact, executed with just three paints – versions of the primaries red, blue and yellow – and three brushes. And rather than using costly sables, the brushes are

all inexpensive and readily available – the 13mm flat listed in the things you will need for this project is actually a pastry brush. If you don't have a similar kitchen utensil, a small household paintbrush will do just as well.

▼ **The curved perspective lines of the platform and roof give a strong sense of depth in this painting.**

FIRST STEPS

1 ▶ Create a frame

Using a propelling pencil and ruler, draw a rectangle measuring 27 x 41cm (10½ x 16in) on your paper. Apply strips of masking tape to define the edges of the picture area. Now start mapping out the composition, beginning with the dramatic sweep of the platform and roof. Rough in the train and the arch at the end of the platform.

2 ▼ Establish the perspective
Put in the main lines of the platforms and roof, making the distance between these lines progressively narrower as they recede from view. Add pockets of detail on the station building.

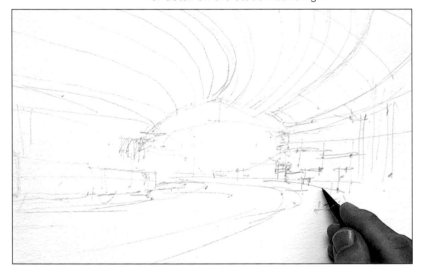

3 ▶ Build up the drawing
Continue building up the detail, paying particular attention to the arch at the end of the platform as the eye will rest here – the literal light at the end of the tunnel. Once the overall structure is correct, turn your attention to the train. Notice how this, too, appears to get smaller as it recedes from view.

4 ▲ Firm up the detail
In this study, the pencil lines form an integral part of the composition, so continue working on the train and the main structure. Don't, however, try to follow the photographs slavishly – the eye can take in only a simplified version of the scene.

DEVELOPING THE PICTURE

With the basic drawing complete, start adding washes of watercolour. The colour in this composition relies heavily on the imagination, so allow yourself to be creative.

5 ▼ **Create atmospheric colours** Using a 25mm (1in) bristle flat brush, make a dilute red-brown mix from equal amounts of the red, blue and yellow, and wash this over the right-hand platform. Mix ultramarine and medium yellow to make a dull green wash and take this over parts of the roof and the opening at the end of the station.

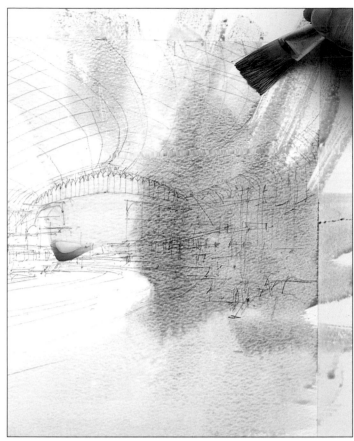

6 ▲ **Add a blue wash** Make a watery blue from the ultramarine and paint this over the right-hand side of your composition, drawing the colour out from the centre. Notice how the paint granulates as the pigment settles on the paper.

7 ▲ **Add a sweep of purple** Use a 13mm (½in) bristle flat brush to sweep a slightly darker wash of ultramarine over the far wall on the left of the painting. Add brilliant red and a touch of medium yellow to the watery ultramarine from step 6 and wash this dilute purple along the length of the tracks. Allow the paint to dry. Now that the background washes are complete, you can remove the masking tape.

TROUBLESHOOTER

REMOVING MASKING TAPE

A danger in removing masking tape is that you will lift off some of the paper at the same time and damage the surface. There is a simple way to avoid this: use a hair-dryer over the masking tape to dry out the sticky resin, then carefully peel the tape off the paper. Now you will have clean, sharp edges to your painting.

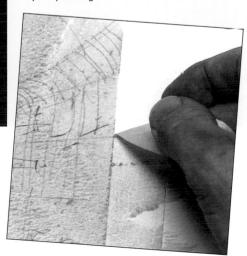

8 ▶ **Start on the train** With the background washes in place, turn your attention to the train. Change to a No. 3 soft round brush and varying mixes of red, blue and yellow to suggest the contours of the carriages, the dark underside wheel area and the windows on the front of the cab. Leave the front of the train white, as though light is catching it.

9 ▲ **Block in the windows** Using a coppery mix of brilliant red and medium yellow, paint the distinctive vertical bands on the front and back of the first carriage. Then block in the windows in a dark blue-grey mixed from ultramarine and a little brilliant red.

10 ▲ **Return to the drawing** The station walls – red brick and dotted with windows – support the vast expanse of roof, itself a complex structure of metal and glass. Once the paint is completely dry, return to your propelling pencil and put in some of these elements, starting with the pattern of windows along the far wall.

11 ◄ **Continue building up detail**
Add to the latticework of struts and supports in the roof, suggest some figures waiting on the right-hand platform and draw several lines of tracks punctuating the centre of the composition and disappearing from view.

Express yourself

Bustling concourse

In this study, the artist used acrylics, starting out with a warm brown background wash, then working up to the lights. The figures are sketched very loosely with a spindly calligraphic style – this gives the impression of the bustling activity on the station concourse.

12 ▼ **Heighten contrasts** Although the intention is to have atmospheric rather than realistic colours, the lights and darks should be roughly accurate. Here, the tracks seem too light in comparison to the rest of the painting. With the 13mm (½in) flat brush, add purple mixed from ultramarine and red over the tracks to darken them. This stronger tone makes the light at the end of the station seem that much brighter.

13 ▲ **Paint figures on the far platform** With the No. 3 soft round brush and the purple mix from step 12, put in windows on the far wall. Add more ultramarine to the purple and squiggle a couple of figures on the platform.

14 ◄ **Add dark accents** Darken the right-hand side of the picture by painting a series of curved purple bands from the roof structure to the platform. Add more brilliant red and water to the mix and paint the shadows and figures along the platform. Emphasize the fact that it extends into the distance by placing dots of dark purple at the far end.

 ◄ **Medium yellow and ultramarine were used on the carriages.**

 ◄ **Medium yellow and brilliant red were used for the details on the train.**

 ◄ **Ultramarine, brilliant red and medium yellow were used for the tracks.**

A FEW STEPS FURTHER

All that's needed now is a final balancing of tones and perhaps a focal point ...

15 ▲ **Build up detail on the right** To strengthen the tonal balance, dab dark purple and a strong reddish-brown on to the shadows on the right of the composition and allow these to dry. Now use your pencil to draw more elements along this right-hand wall. Make these quite sketchy – a suggestion of architectural detail is all that you need.

16 ▲ **Draw the eye into the distance** Strengthen the appearance of the glass structure at the end of the roof by filling in a couple of the panes with purple. These dark touches serve to create a focal point, leading the eye through the station and into the distance.

THE FINISHED PICTURE

A Textural effects
Interesting variegated textural effects are created in the finished picture by the granulation of the ultramarine pigment on the paper.

B Latticework of pencil lines
An intricate pencil drawing forms the basis and body of the painting and provides plenty of detail for the eye to linger on.

C Unpainted areas
The unpainted area in the background suggests the effects of bright light beyond the covered platform and helps to pull the eye into the picture.

Breakfast table

Loose linear brush strokes and dilute washes of watercolour give this simple still life a bright, airy appearance.

Unusually, this painting did not begin with a pencil drawing. Instead, the artist used watercolour in the very first stages – initially to map out the subject in pale blue wash, then to build up the composition with broad strokes and dabs of colour. This direct, unfussy approach set the tone for the rest of the painting.

Colours were kept deliberately pure and clear. Complicated mixtures and subtle combinations were avoided. Instead, the paint was used either unmixed or in washes containing no more than two colours. The colours are generally pale and washy, with just one or two darker tones and shadows introduced in the final stages.

Light and space

Apart from the background, there are no large expanses of colour in the composition. The fruit, flowers and crockery are built up with lots of single brush strokes, applied either as broad lines or as loose, squiggly marks. Plenty of white paper shows through between the freely applied strokes. These empty spaces contribute to the sense of light and space in the picture as a whole.

A relaxed approach

This informal way of painting – described by the artist as 'letting the brush do the work' – is most effective when the whole image is developed simultaneously. Rather than finishing one area, then moving on to the next, work across the painting, building up the colours gradually.

For example, the daffodils were first painted as patches of pale yellow. The artist then went on to block in the fruit and crockery, before returning to the daffodils to add the dark yellow and orange centres.

▶ **Both the drawing and the painting in this still life are done with a brush – linear strokes define the shapes while loose washes fill the larger areas.**

YOU WILL NEED

Piece of 400gsm (200lb) rough watercolour paper 45 x 56cm (18 x 22in)

8 watercolours: cerulean blue; lemon yellow; cadmium yellow; viridian; Prussian blue; ivory black; alizarin crimson; cadmium red

Brushes: Nos. 4 and 6 soft round

Mixing palette, jar of water and kitchen paper for corrections

FIRST STEPS

1 ▶ Paint washy outlines Using a No. 4 soft round brush, make a quick colour sketch in washy cerulean blue – just a few lines are needed to establish the shape and position of each object. Use the tip of the brush to make linear marks and the side of the brush for broader shadows.

2 ▲ Suggest the daffodil blooms Paint the daffodil blooms with loose strokes of washy lemon yellow. Put in the central trumpet of each flower as a blob of strong cadmium yellow.

3 ▲ Paint the apples and pears Change to a No. 6 soft round and paint the apples and pears in a light green mixed from lemon yellow and viridian. Work with broad, free brush strokes, leaving patches of unpainted white paper for the white highlights. Leave the fruit to dry.

DEVELOP THE PICTURE

All the elements have now been established correctly in relation to each other, and you have also indicated the basic colours. It is now time to add the shadows and the background tone.

5 ▲ Paint the shadows Mix a pale wash of Prussian blue and paint each of the shadows around the plate, mug, jug and teapot as a continuous brush stroke. The shadow of the bunch of daffodils is suggested with a loose, squiggly line.

4 ▲ Add the stalks Using the same green wash, paint the daffodil stalks with long, flowing brush strokes. Continue the colour down into the vase to create an impression of transparent glass.

Express yourself
Spontaneous sketch

Still working without a pencil outline, try making a rapid watercolour sketch of a similar still-life subject. Keep mixing to an absolute minimum and use colour spontaneously rather than accurately. For example, here the subject is painted in only four main colours – red, yellow, green and bluish-grey.

7 ▼ Define the apples and pears Change to the No. 4 brush and mix a strong, bright green from viridian and lemon yellow. Use this colour to define the outlines of the fruit and build up their tone. Accentuate the lines around the bottom of the fruit by overpainting them in cadmium yellow.

6 ▲ Add the teapot shadows For the cool shadows on the teapot's handle, spout and lid, mix a pale grey wash by diluting a touch of ivory black with lots of water. Paint another shadow around the body of the teapot, using a sweeping brush stroke to describe its curved form.

8 ◄ Develop the fruit Paint diluted alizarin crimson into the rosy apple, taking the colour over the existing green. Leave a little white paper showing to create a highlight.

▶ **The daffodils are painted in lemon yellow (left), cadmium yellow (top) and an orange (right) mixed from cadmium yellow and cadmium red.**

9 ▼ **Suggest the background** Mix up enough pale grey wash from ivory black and plenty of water to paint the background behind the subject. Using the No. 6 brush, begin to apply the washy grey in loose, scribbly strokes at the top of the picture, leaving an irregular edge around the daffodils.

10 ▼ **Complete the background wash** Continue brushing on the loose grey wash, moving down the picture. Paint around the outlines of the cup and the teapot, leaving a rim of white paper showing around the top edge of each item.

A FEW STEPS FURTHER

The painting needs one or two finishing touches, but no more. At this stage, it is easy to add too much detail and destroy the freshness of the colour and the spontaneity of the brushwork. A few tweaks and a little more background and the painting is complete.

11 ▲ **Extend the background** Using the pale grey wash, define the outline of the teapot once more, so that it stands out as a sharp white shape against the darker background. Continue the wash around the teapot, so that the handle is also defined.

13 ▼ **Add deep shadows** Finally, add the darkest tones to the painting with diluted ivory black. Use this for the shadows on the crockery and vase, and to dot in the dark tones on the fruit.

12 ▲ **Complete the flowers** Change to the No. 4 brush and mix cadmium red and cadmium yellow for the orange centres of the daffodils. These need not be placed accurately – simply dot them on to a few of the flowers.

THE FINISHED PICTURE

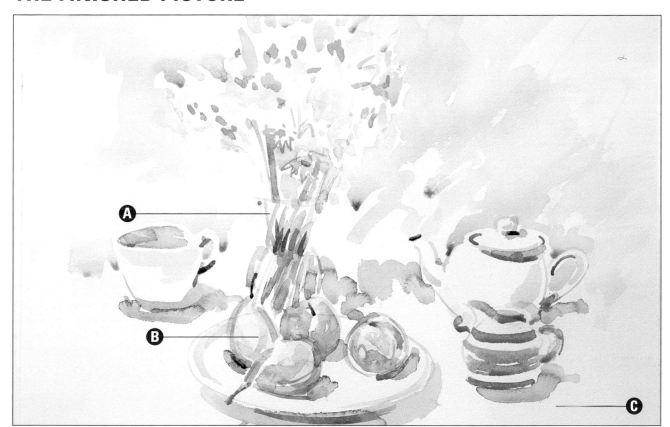

A Glass vase
The transparent vase is defined by the shape of the flower stalks inside it and by the surrounding background tone.

B Fruit colours
Each piece of fruit is created from a broadly painted outline blocked in with loose strokes of colour, which are overlaid in places.

C White table top
The stark whiteness of the unpainted table top contrasts effectively with the brighter colours in the composition.

Inside the rustic kitchen

Break with convention by adding textural interest to your watercolours with scored and scraped lines.

Bristol board is an unusual surface for watercolour painting – it is not generally recommended because it has a smooth, slippery surface on which washes dry unevenly. However, the technique used for this painting – textural marks are scored into the paper with a knife before washes are applied – is itself unorthodox and Bristol board is the ideal surface for this technique.

Scoring the surface

This still life features objects with a variety of textures and patterns. Such an intricate subject can be difficult to paint without overloading the picture with detail, but the artist has overcome this problem by using the scoring method to suggest detail and texture. The technique is like *sgraffito* in reverse – instead of scratching through a painted area to reveal the white paper beneath, you score the paper to make indents in the surface, then apply colour over it.

This process reveals the more absorbent paper beneath the smooth surface coating of the board, so that the scored lines appear darker than the surrounding washes. The channels that are made by the knife, and the bumps which are created by roughing up the surface, become integral parts of the finished painting.

Choice of blade

Almost any type of sharp metal point, such as a penknife, craft knife or scalpel blade, can be used to score the lines, as long as it cuts easily through the board without slipping. A saw-tooth blade dragged across the surface is useful for making hatched and crosshatched lines, and for suggesting rough textures. Always be careful when drawing with a sharp instrument – never place your free hand in the path of your drawing hand.

▶ **Chosen for their textural qualities, the objects in this still life make an ideal subject for the scoring technique.**

Piece of Bristol board
45 x 60 cm (18 x 24in)

Brushes: Nos. 4 and 2 soft
rounds; No. 10 flat wash
brush

9 watercolours: ultramarine;
yellow ochre; burnt umber;
ivory black; sap green;

viridian; alizarin crimson;
cobalt blue; cadmium yellow

Mixing palette or dish

Jar of water

Saw-tooth blade

Penknife, craft knife or
scalpel blade

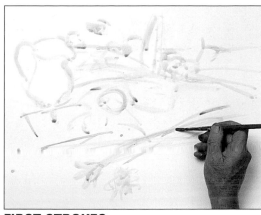

FIRST STROKES

1 ▲ **Draw with a brush** Using a No. 4 soft round
brush, rough in the main outlines of the still-life
group with a dilute wash of ultramarine. Don't
worry too much about accuracy – try to express
the exuberant lines of the subject.

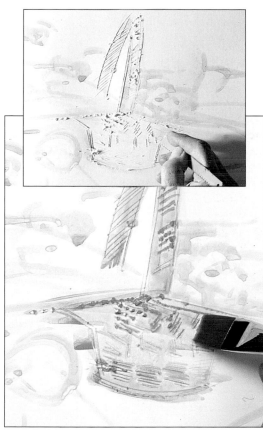

2 ▲ **Paint the basket** Draw the outline of the
basket by scoring the surface of the board
with the sharp point of a saw-tooth blade. Then
suggest the woven pattern of the basket by
scoring short, angular lines into the paper, using
both the point and the teeth of the blade (see
inset). Then mix a wash of yellow ochre and
wash this lightly over the basket with a
No. 10 wash brush. The paint darkens where it
sinks into the indents made by the knife and
catches on the roughened paper. Leave to dry.

DEVELOPING THE PICTURE

It can be difficult to see where the scored lines are on the white board, so the best way to proceed is section by section. Score one area of the picture and paint it before moving on to score and paint the next.

3 ▶ Score and paint
Use the blade to score lines that suggest dried flowers and teasels in the basket. Work around the shapes of the white flowers. Mix a wash of burnt umber and sweep it over the dried flowers. Again, the paint darkens where it sinks into the scored marks.

4 ◀ Score the alliums
With a penknife or craft knife, score fine lines at bottom left to show the allium seed-heads. Scratch tiny parallel lines for the seed capsules. Mix a pale wash from ivory black and ultramarine, and brush over the seed-heads with the wash brush to reveal the delicate stalks and seeds. Allow to dry.

5 ▼ Work on the corn Now change to a saw-tooth blade. Use the tip and teeth to score a series of short zigzag lines into the board to suggest the heads of corn lying next to the allium seed-heads. Brush over the lines with a thin wash of yellow ochre to reveal the scored lines.

6 ▶ Add the thistle stalks Use the knife to score the long corn and thistle stalks. Suggest the texture of the thistle heads by scoring short parallel lines at varying angles. Paint a thin layer of sap green over the stalks with the wash brush. Go over the darker stalks with a wash of viridian, letting the light and dark greens mix loosely.

KNOW THE SCORE

These examples show the range of textural effects you can achieve with scored marks. Thick lines were made with a saw-tooth blade; finer ones with the tip of a penknife.

Heads of corn

Basket weave

Dried flowers

Express yourself
Drawing with a blade

While the scoring technique is used in the step-by-step project to capture intricate detail and texture, it is equally appropriate for simpler, more minimal subject matter. Here, the artist first scored the outlines of the crockery and cutlery, the checks of the tablecloth and the vertical lines in the background. Then he added the washes of watercolour. Finally, when the blue wash was dry, he drew the blade diagonally across it to add a vigorous, lively texture to the background.

7 ▲ Add some purples Paint the red onion in the centre with a purple made from alizarin crimson and cobalt blue, loosely mixed. Let the colour settle in pools of light and dark tone that give form to the onion, and leave a white highlight near the top. Use the same mix to darken the thistle heads.

EXPERT ADVICE
Score draw

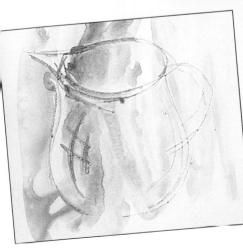

Why not try using the scoring method to 'draw' the outlines of objects? The scored lines are revealed when colour washes are added, and the contrast of soft washes and fine spidery lines is very pleasing – rather like an etching.

8 ▲ Paint the jug Lighten the mixture with more water and use the chisel edge of the wash brush to go over the outlines of the blue jug. Bring out its rounded form with overlaid washes of light and dark tone, applied wet-on-wet.

9 ▲ Bring in more details Use ivory black and cobalt blue to add dark lines to the dried flowers in the basket, and to paint the scored teasels and the shadow on the basket handle. Suggest the pink dried flowers with a sweep of alizarin crimson. Paint the cheese with cadmium yellow. Score circular lines for the texture of the broken bread and wash over it with very dilute burnt umber and ivory black.

A FEW STEPS FURTHER

The painting is now complete, but if you wish you can add just a touch more scratched and painted detail. Resist the temptation to go overboard, though, as you risk losing the spontaneity you have achieved so far.

11 ▶ Scratch back When the washes have dried fully, add texture and highlights to the crusty bread and the skin of the onion by scratching broken lines with the tip of the knife. Then scrape at the unpainted areas left in step 3 to give an impression of the fluffy texture of the white flowers.

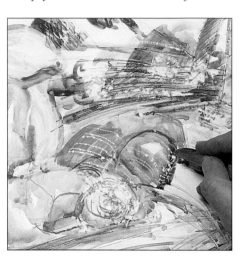

10 ◀ Strengthen the image Continue to work all over the picture, building up local colour and strengthening the dark areas. Using a mixture of alizarin crimson and burnt umber, add warm shadows to the onion and to the basket and its contents. Strengthen the jug with ultramarine, then paint the chopping board with a loose wash of burnt umber. Use viridian and sap green to add more green stalks in the foreground. Leave to dry.

12 ▼ **Add more highlights** In the foreground, use the knife blade to scrape out small patches of colour to suggest the highlights on the thistle heads.

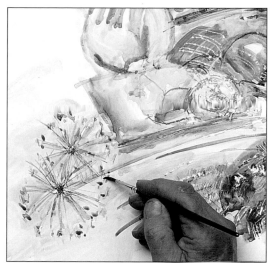

13 ▲ **Add some seeds** Mix burnt umber and a touch of ultramarine, and dot in some seeds around the allium heads, using a No. 2 round brush. Add a few more in alizarin crimson.

THE FINISHED PICTURE

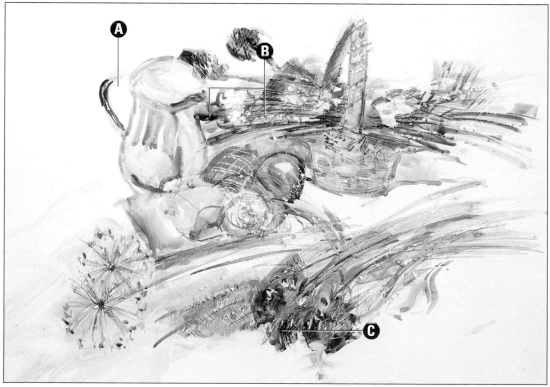

A Lively brushwork
The absence of an initial pencil sketch encouraged freedom and spontaneity in the brushwork.

B Less is more
The white flowers are not really drawn – instead their fluffy texture is registered by scuffing up the paper.

C Surface texture
Scoring and scratching the surface of the board added character to the picture, as well as suggesting more detail and texture.

House plants in watercolour

This striking, close-up composition of three different conservatory plants shows that you do not need a grand subject or broad view to capture the beauty of nature.

Plants offer a particular challenge to the artist. The variety of forms, colours and textures require close observation and a careful choice of colours.

A painting such as this inevitably includes a lot of greens. Although green might appear to be quite a cool, fresh colour, the painting nevertheless manages to evoke the sun-drenched, humid atmosphere of the conservatory.

A range of greens

The trick is to observe the colours to be found in the light and shadowed areas. The artist has captured a wide range of greens, in both warm and cool tones. He utilized a wet-on-wet style occasionally to let the colours run together and gain smoothly blended tones.

Visual editing

When re-creating a scene such as this, you continually need to edit the still life, simplifying the information from the original into something that can be reproduced. You are not trying to make a botanical rendering. What is important is that your painting looks believable, with an accurate representation of the shapes and light. If the composition needs a bit of help, feel free to rearrange the plants or leaves.

▲ **The reds and greens that predominate in this carefully observed study of plants provide an exciting complementary colour contrast.**

FIRST STROKES

1 ▼ **Draw in the pencil outline** Use a 2B pencil to sketch the basic picture on to the paper. Pay special attention to the shapes of the leaves and the overall forms of the plants, as they are the main focus of the composition. Close observation at this stage will pay dividends as the painting progresses.

3 ▼ **Begin adding colour to the leaves** Look for the bluish reflections on the leaves and, using a No. 9 round brush, apply a very thin mix of cerulean blue to these areas. Use the same colour to block in the rounded plant at the front of the picture, as well as the view through the leaves and out of the window. Leave to dry.

2 ▲ **Lay a thin background wash** Leaving the highlights and the brighter parts of the composition blank, apply a very thin wash of yellow ochre and Payne's grey over the entire picture using a No. 10 round brush. Leave the wash to dry.

4 ▲ **Paint the light areas** Add a little lemon yellow to your blue mix to make light green. Apply the paint from top to bottom of each leaf on the large plants. The paint will be most concentrated at the bottom of the leaves, giving the impression of light shining through the paler parts. Develop the rounded plant. The cerulean blue applied in step 3 will show through the green in places, creating a denser colour that contrasts with the translucent blue-lemon mix.

DEVELOPING THE PICTURE

Now that you have put in the palest tones of the leaves, pots and floor tiles, you can begin to build up the medium and dark tones on top. Work wet-in-wet so that the colours run into one another for a natural effect.

5 ▲ **Block in the floor and pots** Mix a light terra-cotta colour, adding a lot of Indian red and a little more yellow ochre to the original ochre mix used in step 2. Changing to a No. 7 round brush, block in the floor and pots. You will need to use this smaller brush in order to cut in around other areas of colour, as it is important that the terra-cotta shade does not 'bleed'. Darken the terra-cotta mix with a little more Indian red and some burnt umber. Apply to the lighter areas of the stems, using a No. 3 round brush.

6 ▲ **Apply the main leaf colour** Mix sap green and lemon yellow to make a more intense lime green. Using a No. 5 round brush, start to develop the detail of the lighter parts of the leaves where the sun catches them. Be very careful to render the shapes accurately.

7 ▲ **Introduce the darker areas** Mix lots of sap green with burnt umber and a little Payne's grey for a rich leaf colour. Add some gum arabic to intensify the colour and enable you to re-wet it once dry. Next, mix a dark stem colour with a little brown madder alizarin and lots of burnt umber. Work across the picture, painting the green mix wet-on-wet over the lime green to create the dark leaf areas. Drop brown colour on to the stems as you work across the painting.

8 ▲ **Continue adding definition to the leaves** Carry on adding the darker colours to all the plants. On the rounded plant, dab on the colour to show the smaller leaves. This adds density to the plants – until now, the painting has been very light and fresh. This stage takes a long time, but do not attempt to rush it, as the effect of the wet-on-wet technique is central to the whole painting. Work methodically across the picture, as you did before.

Express yourself
Pattern of leaves

Leaf shapes and the patterns they create are endlessly fascinating. In this pencil drawing, the artist has focused closely on the foliage of a rubber plant so that the leaves fill the paper. The pattern of leaves is more important here than the structure of the plant itself. A hint of tone and texture is achieved by the lines drawn on the foreground leaves.

9 ▲ Add colour to the pots Mix burnt umber, a little yellow ochre and a little Payne's grey to make a medium brown for the soil and the insides of the pots. Apply with a No. 6 round brush. Add some Indian red to the mix to warm up the shady side of the pots, paying close attention to where the areas of light fall. The warm colours of the pots contribute to the bright, sunny atmosphere of the painting.

10 ▲ Define the areas of shadow Mix sap green, Payne's grey and just a little burnt umber. Use this for the very dark green leaves and stems. As before, work methodically across the paper, introducing the dark brown colour from step 7 occasionally to add variety – use the colours together wet-on-wet.

11 ▲ Complete the areas of shadow Continuing with the dark brown and green mixes, work into all the shadow areas. Stand back and look at your painting. Remember that you are trying to create a believable, evocative picture, not a slavish re-creation of the original, so you can use a bit of artistic licence if necessary. If you feel the painting needs some more areas of shadow, add them, but keep it looking natural.

▲ Adding Payne's grey to the sap green creates a dark green for the shadow areas on the foliage.

12▲ **Embellish the background** Mix Indian red with a little brown madder alizarin. Block in the floor tiles, using the No. 9 round brush – these will make sense of the composition spatially. Add a little ultramarine, and use this mix to add detail to the pots. Make a thin mix of yellow ochre, Payne's grey and brown madder alizarin for the window frames. Paint these in as simple straight lines.

13◀ **Finish off the background** Complete the lines that form the window frames – these provide a suggestion of the setting, but do not detract from the composition's main focus. The painting is now a very believable rendering of plants in a conservatory.

A FEW STEPS FURTHER

All the main areas of light and shadow are now included, but you can improve the picture further by adding more colours to the shadows and intensifying the background.

14 ◀ **Sharpen the picture**
Make a more intense mix of the dark green used on the leaves in step 10. This mix should be almost black. Using the No. 3 brush, cut in around the leaf shapes, adding more definition and sharpening up the picture. Add further accents to the pots to emphasize the light and dark areas and to strengthen the effect of bright sunlight. Make sure that you have represented all the areas of intense shadow, even the very fine ones. For close work, change to a No. 3 flat brush.

15 ▲ **Suggest the background** Mix sap green and cerulean blue. Apply using the No. 6 round brush to give a suggestion of foliage outside the conservatory. This increases the sense of depth in the picture and helps the painting to look more complete.

THE FINISHED PICTURE

A Wide tonal range
To convey the impression of strong sunlight filtering through the window and plants, a wide range of tones was used, both on the leaves and the pots.

B Simple background
In contrast to the busy subject matter in the picture's foreground, the background was kept uncluttered – the windows and floor tiles are suggested very simply.

C Dark shadows
The areas of deepest shadow on the plants were painted during the final stages. The dark colour crisply defines the lighter shapes of the leaves.

Sunlight and shadows

Watercolour is an ideal medium for capturing the subtle colours and shapes of shadows created by sunlight filtering into an interior.

What brings an interior to life? The subject matter certainly does – the room needs to have interesting objects, decoration and furniture, and these should complement each other well. The composition is also crucial – everything you choose to include should sit pleasingly within the frame. One of the most overlooked aspects of interiors, however, is the lighting.

Light and dark

In this painting, direct sunshine creates an interesting play of light and dark, with its strong shadows and bright highlights. The sunlight illuminates the right wall, yet leaves the far one in darkness. The artist has exaggerated this contrast

of tone and also the contrast of colour it creates – the warmer browns of the sunlit areas beautifully offset the deeper bluish shadowed areas.

Capturing shadow areas

Key to achieving interesting, variegated shadows is layering the washes, smudging the paint while it is still wet to give a soft, uneven look that mimics the effect of shadows in real life.

As you progress with the layers of colour in the darkest area of the room – the alcove – the paint will become thicker, but you can add drops of water to dilute the wet paint already applied and thus make sections of the wall less opaque. A similar effect can be achieved with some well-judged rubbing back with damp cotton wool. Varying the tone in this way creates lively and realistic shadows. Remember, however, that you have to work quickly.

It is important to alter the colours as well as the tones in the shadow areas – for instance, halfway down the alcove, the artist added more brown to capture light reflected from the warm table.

Before building up the shadow areas, however, it pays to establish the small details you wish to retain, such as the pictures and the items on the table, in the initial stages. This then enables you to focus on the bigger picture – the overall sense of light and shadow in the room. You can return to the details in the very last stages of the painting.

▶ **Soft wet-on-wet washes in the shadows contrast with the crisp lines of the furniture in this atmospheric painting of an interior.**

Piece of 300gsm (140lb)
hot-pressed watercolour paper
38 x 27cm (15 x 10½in)

4B pencil

11 watercolours: carmine;
cadmium scarlet; indigo;
aureolin; yellow ochre;
ultramarine; Payne's grey;
cadmium yellow pale;
cadmium red light;

monestial green; Prussian blue

Watercolour brushes: Nos. 4, 2,
8, 1, 0 rounds

Mixing dish or palette

Jar of water

Masking fluid and an old
No. 4 round brush

Cotton wool and cotton bud

White gouache

FIRST STROKES

1 ▶ Sketch the room
Using a 4B pencil,
mark the outline of
everything in the
room. (Note that to
attain a strong sense
of recession, the
artist used a slightly
different viewpoint
than the one in the
photo on the left.)
Delineate the shape
of the alcove carefully,
as this area is a major
focus of the painting.
The other key objects
that should be well
defined are the chair
and table. Draw the
items on the table
carefully, too, marking
in the clock face.

**2 ◀ Paint and mask
the poppies** Mix
carmine and cadmium
scarlet to create a
bright, warm red. Fill
in the poppies using
a No. 4 brush – don't
worry about definition
at this stage. Once
the red paint has
dried, apply masking
fluid over it with an
old No. 4 round brush.
This will protect the
flowers against being
affected by the other
colours you will be
using around them.

3 ▶ Paint the small objects Using a No. 2 brush, mix an indigo/aureolin wash for the vase and poppy leaves. Smudge the leaves with damp cotton wool. For the bottles, mix yellow ochre with ultramarine. When dry, lighten the far bottle with aureolin. Mix cadmium scarlet, ultramarine and yellow ochre to outline the clock. Add ultramarine and Payne's grey for the picture frame.

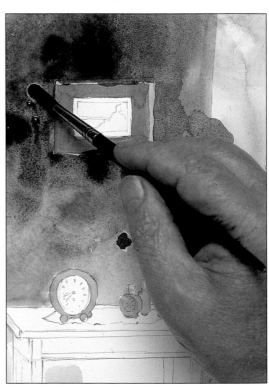

▲ **The artist worked from a portable, self-contained watercolour set which is ideal if you're painting on-site.**

4 ▼ Wash the right-hand wall Mix yellow ochre and cadmium yellow pale. Using a No. 8 brush, wash over the floor and right-hand wall. While the paint is still wet, rub back the light area above the chair with damp cotton wool.

5 ▶ Paint the alcove Add cadmium red light and ultramarine to the mix used in step 4 and paint the top of the right-hand wall wet-on-wet. Create an aubergine colour by adding carmine and a little more ultramarine to this mix. Work over the alcove. Add indigo, Payne's grey and more carmine to the mix and drop it on to the wash with a watery brush. Where the wall joins the alcove, smudge the paint with damp cotton wool.

DEVELOPING THE PICTURE

Complete the main washes by lightly blocking in the table and rug. Then focus your attention on the chair and table, applying paint, then smudging it with damp cotton wool.

6 ▶ Define the chair Paint the skirting board in a pale wash of ultramarine with a little carmine. Make a dilute wash of ultramarine and yellow ochre and wash this pale shade over the table. Then mix carmine and yellow ochre and fill in the rug. Allow to dry. Mix a dark brown from indigo, cadmium red light and yellow ochre and, using the No. 2 brush, start to define the chair.

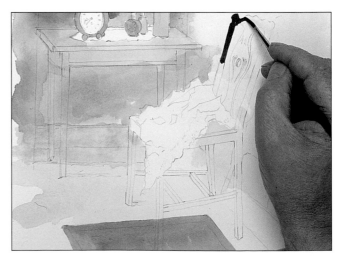

7 ▶ Smudge the paint
Use a more dilute dark brown wash for the lower part of the chair. Add cadmium scarlet and yellow ochre to the mix and apply this warmer brown to the chair-back where the light hits it. With damp cotton wool, gently smudge the paint on the chair.

8 ◀ Add the chair's shadow Use the dark brown mix to paint the table top and legs. Rub back with damp cotton wool, allow to dry and reapply the paint. While still wet, gently rub back once more. Mix ultramarine and yellow ochre, and, with the good No. 4 brush, paint in the shadow of the chair. If the colour looks too dark, rub back with a piece of damp cotton wool.

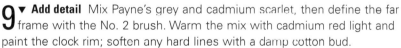

9 ▼ Add detail Mix Payne's grey and cadmium scarlet, then define the far frame with the No. 2 brush. Warm the mix with cadmium red light and paint the clock rim; soften any hard lines with a damp cotton bud.

10 ▶ Build up shadows Use monestial green for the perfume bottle lid. Wash an ultramarine/yellow ochre mix over the clock face. Mix Payne's grey with cadmium scarlet and a little ultramarine. Using the No. 8 brush, wash over the top of the alcove, thinning the colour as you work downwards. Squeeze a few drops of water from a piece of cotton wool over the wet paint on the wall.

Express yourself
Paint another room

This corner of a bedroom, casually strewn with clothing and jewellery, has been treated in the same way as the step by step picture. Diffused dark grey on the shadowed wall contrasts with pale ochre on the lit back wall, the two colours merging where the walls meet.

BLOW GENTLY

TROUBLESHOOTER

Using a small hair-dryer is a great way to speed up the drying process. It allows you to overlay wash on wash without fear of the colours running together. But be sure to use a low setting – if the force coming from the dryer is too strong it could accidentally blow paint across the paper.

11 ▲ **Add more detail** Apply a mix of cadmium red light, yellow ochre and Prussian blue to the top of the right-hand wall. Smudge with damp cotton wool. Wash the area around the table with a mix of yellow ochre and ultramarine, then smudge with damp cotton wool. Make various brown and beige mixes of yellow ochre, cadmium scarlet and ultramarine; using the No. 4 brush, define the main features of the two paintings.

12 ▲ **Strengthen shadows** Using a mid-beige mix from step 11, strengthen the tone on the floor. Paint the wall behind the chair, too, leaving the area above and to the left of the chair unpainted. Dip the brush in water and tap a few drops on to the painted area to add visual interest.

13 ▲ **Refine the shadows** Using the No. 2 brush, paint the shadows in the folded cloth on the chair with a weak mix of ultramarine and a touch of carmine. Mix indigo, yellow ochre and cadmium red light, and use the No. 8 brush to wash over the shadowy area under the table. With a weaker mix, paint the shadow of the chair on the floor and strengthen the wall shadow. Mix yellow ochre and ultramarine to create dark brown; using the No. 2 brush, define the edges of the table and chair.

14 ◄ **Apply greens** Mix aureolin, indigo and a little cadmium red light and paint over the vase with the No. 4 brush. Add a touch of indigo to make a darker green and apply to the foliage. Dilute this colour with water and apply around the foliage to create a halo-like shadow.

15 ▲ **Add finishing touches** Mix yellow ochre, cadmium red light and a tiny speck of Prussian blue, and apply with the No. 8 brush to the large picture frame. Leave to dry. Mix Payne's grey and cadmium red light to make a near-black, and go over the picture frame again.

16 ► **Enhance the details** Mix indigo, yellow ochre and carmine, and use the No. 8 brush to darken the rug. Rub away the masking fluid from the poppies with your fingertip. Mix carmine and cadmium scarlet and paint over them with the No. 4 brush, but don't cover the original colour completely. Use dilute Payne's grey and a No. 1 brush to show the markings on the chair back.

A FEW STEPS FURTHER

The picture now has a moody sense of shadow and light. As the painting focuses on the chair and table top, it makes sense to add a few final details to this area.

17 ▲ **Work on the fabric** Paint the clock face and hands in Payne's grey, then shade the clock face with dilute ultramarine and yellow ochre. Also add shading to the perfume bottles. Mix ultramarine and Payne's grey and, using a No. 1 brush, dot paint along the fabric edge to suggest eyelets. Using a No. 0 brush, draw tassels in white gouache.

18 ▲ **Dribble paint** Mix very dilute cadmium scarlet and cadmium yellow pale. With the No. 8 brush, tap a few drops of paint in the less detailed areas of the painting to create a lively picture surface. Tilt the paper to allow the paint to trickle down.

THE FINISHED PICTURE

A Coloured shadows
By using a palette of deep purples applied in layered washes, a very effective sense of late-afternoon shadow has been built up on the alcove wall.

B Focusing the eye
The crumpled fabric lying on the chair was left unpainted. Its dazzling whiteness creates a compelling focal point among the deep shadows that engulf the room.

C Spattered paint
The finishing touches of spattered and dripped red and yellow paint add a sense of excitement and drama to what might otherwise appear a rather sombre scene.